Anonymous

The Chartist riots at Newport : November, 1839

Anonymous

The Chartist riots at Newport : November, 1839

ISBN/EAN: 9783337304799

Printed in Europe, USA, Canada, Australia, Japan

Cover: Foto ©ninafisch / pixelio.de

More available books at **www.hansebooks.com**

THE
CHARTIST RIOTS
AT
NEWPORT.

NOVEMBER, 1839.

SECOND EDITION.

Newport:
W. N. JOHNS, PRINTER AND PUBLISHER, "STAR" OFFICES
1889.

CONTENTS.

	Page.
THE OLD WESTGATE HOTEL (*Frontispiece*)	
NEWPORT A CENTURY AGO ...	6
SIX POINTS OF THE CHARTER ...	8
ROYAL OAK NEWPORT (*Illustration*) ...	8
THE LEADERS:	
JOHN FROST (*Portrait*)	9
ZEPHANIAH WILLIAMS (*Portrait*)...	11
WILLIAM LLOYD JONES (*Portrait*)	12
CONDITION OF MONMOUTHSHIRE	13
WAGES EARNED	13
THE CHARTIST PROPAGANDA	13
THE CONVENTION	14
THE AUTHORITIES WAKING UP	16
APPREHENSION OF HENRY VINCENT	17
THE CRISIS APPROACHING	18
GATHERING OF FORCES ...	19
SCENE AT BLACKWOOD...	20
PROCEEDINGS AT NANTYGLO	22
JONES AT ABERSYCHAN ...	24
FURTHER PROGRESS OF JOHN FROST ...	27
THE WELSH OAK (*Illustration*)	28
LAWLESSNESS OF WILLIAMS'S FORCE	29
PREPARATIONS AT NEWPORT ...	32
DANGEROUS RECONNOITRING ...	35
THE MILITARY CALLED OUT	36
THE MARCH INTO NEWPORT ...	37
ATTACK UPON THE WESTGATE ...	39
AFTER THE CONFLICT .	43

CONTENTS.

	Page.
PERSONAL EXPERIENCES	45
APPREHENSION OF LEADERS	46
ISRAEL FIRMAN (*Portrait*)	49
TRIALS OF THE PRISONERS (*Illustration*)	50
SENTENCES	64
MISCELLANEOUS CHARGES	65
OPINION OF THE JUDGES	66
SIR JOHN CAMPBELL'S OPINION	66
REMISSION OF CAPITAL SENTENCES	67
REMOVAL OF THE PRISONERS	67
DESTINATION OF THE PRISONERS	67
IN MEMORIAM	67
MONMOUTH GAOL (*Illustration*)	68
PRISONERS PARDONED	69
REVIEW OF THE TRIAL	70
PRESENTATION TO SIR THOMAS PHILLIPS	70
SIR THOMAS PHILLIPS (*Portrait*)	71
CHARTIST ANECDOTES	71
SAVED BY A DREAM	72
CHARTIST HAT	72
REMINISENCES OF DR. PRICE, LLANTRISSENT	72
DISCOVERY OF BULLETS	74

THE
CHARTIST RIOTS
AT NEWPORT.

1839.

THE OLD WESTGATE HOTEL.

THE wide recognition accorded to Newport as an outlet for the vast mineral resources of the eastern portion of South Wales has almost completely overshadowed the notoriety previously attached to the town by the unfortunate circumstances which occurred in its midst just half a century ago.

After the construction of the spacious docks, and extended railways, whereby Newport became much enlarged, and the activity apparent in its thoroughfares vastly increased, few visitors to the place found a more attractive object for their close inspection than the old Westgate Hotel. While the ancient Norman Church on Stow Hill, and the Edwardian Castle on the Usk, would be merely glanced at, the quaint old hostelry, standing conspicuously in the centre of the town, would receive a degree of attention which its architectural features by no means merited. Oft has the stranger been seen gazing intently at the building, evidently conjuring up in his imagination the scenes enacted on the 4th November, 1839, when, as the frontispiece represents, a large mob of excited Chartists attacked the place, and were repulsed by the steady gallantry of a few soldiers, who, from the front bay of the eastern window facing the square, poured a destructive fire into the midst of the masses assembled. Recovering from his reverie, the stranger would curiously quiz the two pillars supporting the porch of the doorway, and note by the holes which perforated them from side to side the course of the bullets fired by the attacking party at the special constables and others, who offered a timorous defence at the entrance; and then, anon, peer into the lobby to discern, hanging on the walls, some old paintings through which the destructive missiles had also passed.

Apart from the incidents connected with the Chartist Riots, the old Westgate Hotel had no history, and possessed no feature, making it a matter of regret that the building has given place to a new structure more commensurate with public requirements and the exacting demands of modern society.

NEWPORT A CENTURY AGO.

What a change in the condition of Newport does the period of a century represent! A hundred years ago the river Usk at Newport was crossed not by a substantial stone bridge, but by a ricketty old structure resting on wooden piles, the flooring being loose boards held in their places by pegs, and so arranged as to offer no resistance to the rising tide. The Castle was no less a conspicuous object of ruin than it had been since the last Civil War, or than it now appears. The town contained only about two hundred houses and 750 inhabitants. The principal street led from the Bridge to St. Woolos Church, which edifice also presented a very neglected condition. The graveyard was open to the public, and contained the parish stocks. Sunday games, after Divine Service, were not obsolete; and on Thursday in Whitsun week, when Stow Fair was held, its sacred precincts were unceremoniously invaded by boisterous pleasure-seekers, and those who bought and sold. The Market, situate in the middle of High Street, was so disgracefully dilapidated that the Marquis of Worcester was repeatedly presented at the Quarter Sessions for not repairing it. The Bull-ring still existed in front of it. Cattle coming into the town, over the Bridge, were taxed; and a huge board, affixed to the wall of the Bridge Inn Stables, and which until within the last few years remained *in situ*, indicated the toll per head which could be levied. The Town Pill ran up from the river nearly to High Street, where the low thatch-covered houses were ranged so closely together as to leave a space of not more than eleven feet in width for the roadway, down which Her Majesty's Mail Coach came rattling once a day, some twenty-six hours after leaving London. Neither Railways, Canals, or Docks had been constructed; and the inhabitants of the town were not privileged to enjoy either the conveniences of gas or a copious supply of pure water in their houses. The iron trade of the district was in its infancy, only three furnaces then existing in the county, the make of which was 2,000 tons a year. Coal was brought down to small craft in the river by mule-packs, the total shipments reaching about 100 tons per week. The town was governed by a Mayor, Aldermen, and Common Council, the Mayor in 1789 being one Richard Griffiths. A Town Hall is spoken of in the old record, but where it was situate is now forgotten. Justice was here administered in Quarter Sessions, after the fashion of the times (a privilege which the borough has since lost), an illustration of which we may quote : In the year 1777, at a Quarter Sessions held on June 10, a woman, named Alice Morgan, was indicted for the felony of breaking down a hedge, and, being found guilty, was sentenced to be stripped from her waist upwards and whipped, at twelve o'clock, at the whipping-post in the borough with thirty lashes, till the blood issued forth, and that she be sent in the meanwhile to the Clock House in the borough. The Clock House at that period was a portion of the west gate of the borough, and stood between the Bon Marché and the Westgate Hotel, separating High Street from Stow Hill, anciently called Church Street, then forming the only entrance to the town from the west. The structure, when no longer required for defence of the town, was appropriated to the temporary confinement of prisoners, the narrow apartment over the arch which crossed the roadway being used for the purpose. Access was gained by a short flight of steps on the left side.* In 1798 this apartment, and the steps leading to it, was, by order of a parish meeting held at a public-house called the Old Sloop—known to the present generation as the Market Boat, Stow Hill—ordered to be taken down that the other part of the structure might be repaired. The work, after being taken in hand, proved a more expensive job than was anticipated, and the desired improvement came to a standstill. Charles Morgan, Esq., however, solved the difficulty. For the purpose of enlarging the entrance to the town where the gateway stood, he proposed to remove the old structure, and build a proper and sufficient Prison in Mill Street, the conditions being that he was to have the materials of the old Prison Gateway, the ground on which it stood, and a sum of £40 from the town exchequer. The conditions were agreed to, and the Gateway was swept away, and with it also a portion of a house called the Old Westgate Inn, a remnant of which is still represented by the butcher's shop in Baneswell Road, occupied by Mr. F. Carter.

Following this improvement there can be no doubt that the Westgate Hotel—so well known to the present generation—was soon erected, and magnificent and spacious at that period in so small a town must the new building have appeared. As a commercial hotel it always did a good business, but in later years its accommodation for public or large festive gatherings proved inadequate. Many a gay and brilliant party, however, gathered under its roof ; and numerous have been the ecclesiastical, military, and civic dignitaries who there quaffed the choice wines and spirits, of which the late landlord always maintained a good store. Mr. Samuel Thompson Hallen, who by accident met with his death in 1883, and whose widow still survives, occupied the hotel for a period of nearly 50 years, and therefore was landlord at the time of the Riots.

---

* On the demolition of the old Westgate Hotel, a portion of these steps was discovered to have been enclosed in the building at the time of its erection.

THE CHARTER.

Of the origin and nature of the political movement, commonly known as Chartism, it will not be necessary to say much, nor will it be desirable to canvas the merits of the views so zealously advocated by its supporters. It will be sufficient to state here that a very extensive political agitation existed for the purpose of obtaining legislative sanction to what were termed "Six Points" of the so-called "Charter," namely, Universal Suffrage, Equal Electoral Districts, Vote by Ballot, Annual Parliaments, Abolition of Property Qualification, and Payment of Members. These points were demanded by legislation, and failing thus to obtain them, the supporters of the agitation resolved to bring about their adoption by force and violence.

THE LEADERS.

One of the most able, earnest, and eloquent advocates for the Charter was Henry Vincent, a printer by trade, who "stumped" the country in expounding the principles to which he adhered. He visited Monmouthshire, and, "on the Hills," obtained many zealous followers. At Newport he delivered some inflammatory speeches, for which he was apprehended, and committed to prison on a charge of sedition.

Amongst those who were subsequently brought into greater prominence than others were John Frost, of Newport; Zephaniah Williams, of Coalbrook Vale; and William Jones, of Pontypool.

John Frost was a native of Newport, and is said to have been born on the 25th of May, 1786, at the Royal Oak Inn, Thomas Street, a house which was the property of his father. This house was demolished in order to effect an enlargement of the Post Office in 1884. Frost lost his father while yet a youth, but his mother survived the events which brought both to her and other members of the family so much grief. The care of young Frost principally devolved upon his paternal grandfather, a boot and shoe maker, then residing in Newport, who intended to bring him forward so as to be capable of succeeding to the business. The boy was ultimately apprenticed to a tailor, at Cardiff, when about 16 years of age; but it was found that he devoted more time to desultory reading than to the making of shoes, an occupation which had no charms for him. Before the period of his apprenticeship had expired, young Frost went to Bristol. Recommended by his uncle, a Mayor of Newport, he obtained a situation as assistant to a woollen draper, and so qualified himself for the business that, when he reached the age of 20, he had no difficulty in finding employment in London, at the establishment of a tailor and draper. Whilst assiduous in his duties, he studied much, and frequented debating societies, then well-known in London, at which also attended men of some

notoriety in the political world. From London, Frost returned to his native town at the earnest solicitation of his mother, and became the possessor of a prosperous business. Mr. Frost commenced business in Newport as a tailor and draper, in the year 1811, in a house belonging to his stepfather, near the Royal Oak, Mill Street. Shortly after this he married a widow named Geach, who, with her two children, resided with her uncle, Mr. William Foster, a member of the old Corporation, and Mayor of the Borough of Newport in the years 1804, 1812, and 1817. At Mr. Foster's demise, Mrs. Frost and her children derived a handsome property. By Mr. Frost she became the mother of two sons

JOHN FROST.

and five daughters. About the year 1822 Mr. Frost, after a frequent perusal of the works of Paine and Cobbett, first displayed aspirations to rank as a public writer, and pamphleteering was a favourite mode of showing his hostility to what he deemed public abuses. In a dispute between the Burgesses of Newport and the Corporation respecting the Marshes, Mr. Frost sided with the Burgesses, contending that the property was unjustly held from them. His action in this matter gained him golden opinions. He also took an active part with the Burgesses in litigation with the Duke of Beaufort, and at all contested elections of the period proved himself an active partizan. His uncontrollable spirit led him into a quarrel with Mr. Prothero, Town Clerk for the Borough, and agent to Sir Charles Morgan. Frost, through accepting bail for a relative, became involved, and the threats which he made of exposing Mr. Prothero was construed into an attempt to extort money. Fearing the result of legal proceedings, Frost sold off his stock, and paid all his creditors except one relative, who had him arrested for a debt of £200. Frost thereupon declared himself insolvent, and suffered a remand for six months. An action for libel was subsequently brought against him by Mr. Prothero, and he was sent to Coldbath Fields Prison for six months. On his return to Newport he was received more like a hero than a criminal. From this period, though he once more went into business, he became a leading local politician, and displayed great bitterness against those from whom he differed.

Mr. Frost was an early convert to the cause of the Chartists, and his earnest advocacy and strong expression of language soon got him into trouble. His prosecution for libel and committal to prison tended to increase his popularity, and brought him more into public favour. He was elected one of the Council of the Borough at the close of 1835, when the Municipal Corporation Act was carried into effect, and was re-elected in 1838, when his first term of office expired. He was also a Poor-Law Guardian. After a full investigation into his character and past conduct, and with the knowledge that he had been imprisoned for libel, he was recommended to the King by the Secretary of State for the Home Department for appointment as one of the Justices of the Peace for the Borough. His name was in due course entered upon the Commission, and, while he held the office, is said to have performed the duties appertaining to it with diligence, zeal, independence, and impartiality. In November, 1836, Mr. Frost was elected to fill the civic chair, and during his year of office, as Mayor, it was his privilege and honour to proclaim in the Borough the Accession of Queen Victoria. In the performance of his public duties it was generally recognised that he acted with becoming dignity. Impartially speaking, he was a man held in great respect, not only by his fellow-townsmen, but throughout the district where he was widely known.

In stature Mr. Frost stood about 5ft. 7in. in height, and was rather stoutly formed. The expression of his countenance is described as mild and thoughtful; and his general appearance altogether at variance with recklessness or violence of conduct. His manner was regarded as indicating more than usual benevolence and kindliness of disposition. His tone of voice, both in conversation and when speaking in public, was pleasing and conciliatory. At the time of the Riots, in 1839, Mr. Frost must have been over 50 years of age, and therefore beyond the influence of youthful imperiosity.

Mr. Frost for many years lived in Murenger House, and afterwards at 55, High Street.

ZEPHANIAH WILLIAMS.

Of Zephaniah Williams little is known, and he appears to have been a man who took no prominent part in any public questions until the agitation, respecting the People's Charter, commenced. At the time of the Riots he was the keeper of a beerhouse, called the Royal Oak, at Coalbrook Vale, about 21 miles from Newport. He had apparently no less zeal, if less discretion, than John Frost, and exercised great influence among the toiling masses who dwelt in the district, and was capable of arousing in them no small amount of enthusiasm. Respect for law he had none, and for religion less. The fear of punishment for infringing the laws of man was sufficiently powerful to ensure a nominal acquiescence; but the consequences of disobedience to the laws of God appeared to him more remote, and therefore he utterly disregarded them. In short, he had no belief in God or eternity.

A local and friendly Bard thus represents Williams's sentiments, in describing a visit he paid to John Frost in his cell after being condemned :—

> Deem'st thou . . . it is well to live
> In misery—without thy liberty—
> From day to day in this infernal jail,
> Where none but felons dwell, nor man is seen,
> Save only some grim-faced janitor?

Nor ever woman with her smile can cheer
Thy soul—*soul there be in man or woman!*
Wilt thou remain in such a hell as this,
When, with "a bare bodkin" or some small drop
Of liquid poison, thou canst end thy woe,
And find in sleep an everlasting rest,
From which there is no waking?
      We have come
To tell thee that we choose to die,—not live
To please our enemies, in prison gloom
Where never ray appears of sunny joy.

WILLIAM LLOYD JONES.

William Lloyd Jones (as he designated himself in later years), or William Jones (as he pleaded when arraigned for high treason), was the illegitimate son of a tradesman at Bristol. At an early age he left his home, and abandoned his trade of watchmaker for the "Stage," where he came to be looked upon as a "fine bould player," his voice being well-toned and flexible, his cast of features good, his figure commanding, and his assurance irrepressible. His fame in this direction, however, never rose higher than the plaudits of a stroller's booth. About the year 1833 Jones was induced by a widow named Harvey, living at Pontypool, to undertake the management of the watchmaking business of her late husband, and this he continued to do until he married a Miss Edwards, of Abergavenny, and started in business on his own account. Shortly after this he was charged by his late employer with embezzlement, but, as the defalcations had been made a debt, the prosecution failed. When the Charter was first advocated in Pontypool, Jones readily gave the cause the support of his talents and character, and continued until the last a "physical force" advocate.

CONDITION OF MONMOUTHSHIRE.

The condition of Monmouthshire and the character of its population, at this period, were favourable to disorder and crime. The mineral riches of the mountain district had begun to be developed, and large numbers of people were attracted from distant parts—people who were mostly ignorant, and for whom, neither in a religious or moral point of view, was adequate provision made. Still, employment being plentiful and wages high, there were no privations or wretchedness arising from poverty. In the course of subsequent prosecutions of prisoners charged with riot, the late Mr. Samuel Homfray, then proprietor of Tredegar Iron Works, stated that the following were the wages paid to the men of that establishment. where 5,000 men were employed :—

Colliers and Miners	22/- to 24/-	per week.
Furnacemen	30/-	,,
Puddlers and Heaters	35/-	,,
Rollers	50/- to 60/-	,,
Fitters, Smiths, and Patternmakers	25/-	,,
Carpenters	21/-	,,
Moulders	24/-	,,
Masons	24/-	,,
Labourers	2/- to 2/4	per day.

The people were, however, readily influenced by men who glibly declaimed against injustice and tyranny. Sir Thomas Phillips, in writing of the people of Brynmawr and Beaufort, states that the morals of the people were deplorably low. Drunkenness, blasphemy, indecency, sexual vices, and lawlessness widely prevailed. This district was one of the chief sources of Chartism. Neither Church nor School had been established by those who employed the people or owned the land. The Report of the Education Commissioners, who made an enquiry after the Riots had taken place, stated that "demoralisation was everywhere dominant, and all good influences comparatively powerless in the district."

It was under such conditions, and amid such population, that the Chartist movement took root and flourished in the district.

THE CHARTIST PROPAGANDA.

In October, 1838, an active propagandism of Chartism was

initiated in the district. On Tuesday evening, the 23rd, a meeting was held at the Bush Inn, Newport, when Mr. Frost attended. The Charter was explained in Welsh to those present, and a public meeting arranged for. This was held at the great room of the Parrot Hotel, when Mr. Frost presided. In the course of his address he characterised the Reform Bill of 1831 as humbug, and equally denounced both Whigs and Tories. He alleged that if the Charter became law, honest men would be put into the House of Commons, and they would repeal all bad laws and enact none but good ones. The prevailing distress, he urged, was produced by bad government, and induced a demand for further reform.

In the beginning of 1839 a Convention assembled in London, composed of delegates principally of the working classes from various towns in the kingdom. After a free expression of opinions by the leaders, it became evident to the nation that they were little better than a band of anarchists, and attention was given by the authorities to all their movements. The appearance of Mr. Frost in the Convention was an exceptional circumstance, for he held Her Majesty's Commission as Justice of the Peace, and was the only Englishman in the assembly who held a like appointment. The attention of the authorities was called to the fact, and the responsible Minister of the Crown taunted in respect to the appointment. When it was reported to Lord John Russell that Mr. Frost had attended a meeting at Pontypool, where violent and inflammatory language had been used, his Lordship interrogated Mr. Frost by letter, in which he stated that if the allegations were true, "it must cause your name to be erased from the Commission of the Peace for the County of Monmouth." The reply of Mr. Frost was characteristically defiant. After reminding his Lordship that he was "not a Magistrate for the County of Monmouth, but for the Borough of Newport," he observed : "Whether your Lordship will retain my name, or cause it to be erased, is to me a matter of perfect indifference, for I set no value on an office dependent for its continuance, not according to the mode in which its duties are performed, but on the will of a Secretary of State." He denied that he had used violent and inflammatory language, and contended that he ought not to be made answerable for the language uttered by others, adding, "If these are to be the terms on which Her Majesty's Commission of the Peace are to be holden, take it back again, for surely none but the most servile of men would hold it on such terms."

Mr. Frost, by his defiant conduct, obtained still greater popularity, and, early in March, a public dinner was organized in London by his friends, as a testimony of their appreciation of his spirited rebuke of the Secretary of State's interference in the free expression of public opinion.

The Convention resolved to send "missionaries" to different parts of the kingdom to agitate for the Charter, and Mr. Frost was elected to act as one. He declined to serve, but in other ways continued the agitation. The terms of the Charter were issued from the office of the *Weekly Despatch*, "beautifully printed in blood colour, and adapted to hang up in every public-house and cottage;" while the *Weekly Chronicle* deemed the members of the Convention as bloodthirsty and desperate a set of men as any which the French Revolution in its worst days produced. At another meeting held in London, at which Mr. Frost presided, threats of violence were used; and before the close of March it was announced that his name had been obliterated from the Commission of the Peace.

One of the earliest public meetings was held in the county town of Monmouth on Saturday, 26th March, and was attended by two "missionaries," appointed by the Convention, named Vincent and Burns. Both political parties were denounced—one as full-fed Tories; their opponents, the Whigs, as hungry bloodhounds. On the following Tuesday, the 29th, the "missionaries" attended Newport, and delivered addresses in Pentonville, when Vincent referred to the snowball of Chartism being rolled up the hill and let down as an avalanche upon the aristocracy of the land.

Special meetings were held to enlist females in the cause, and on the 1st of April, after a females' tea party at the Ship and Pilot Inn, Vincent proceeded towards Pentonville, followed by a mob of howling Chartists, who are said to have made the welkin ring with most horrible yells and noises. In a speech replete with oaths, he declared, by the God who made the Tories, and by the God who made the Radicals, they were determined to carry the Charter, and, if necessary, resort to physical force. On Wednesday evening, in the same place, he invoked the people to arm and be prepared against the 6th May, intimating that if the Charter were not conceded, every hill and valley should send forth its armed force to extort the terms propounded. He called upon the people to swear that they would be ready to act, and his appeal was answered by shouts of "We swear! we swear!" He then called on all those who were ready to turn out to hold up their arm, and a majority of those present did so. One Edwards, exhibiting his, said "Here's the stuff." Vincent returned to the Ship and Pilot to meet another gathering of ladies. Mr. Edward Thomas conjured the gentlemen not to intrude, but to leave the ladies altogether to Mr. Vincent.

The agitation was now general throughout the country, and the people became much agitated. At Devizes there was a conflict between the Chartists and the authorities, and at Radstock the Chartist leaders were attacked by the people, and had to fly for their lives. Much interest was felt in a Meeting at Stroud, at which Mr. John Frost attended by special leave of the Convention to oppose Lord John Russell. There was a gathering of 10,000 people, but no great disorder resulted. A few days subsequently a large meeting was held at Pontypool, when a man named Edwards, a baker of Newport, was introduced as the "lion" of the evening. Wm. Lloyd Jones occupied the chair. Edwards, in the course of his remarks, said he would not give a tinker's damn for any Chartist who would not stand to have his head cleft asunder in support of the Charter, and that every Whig and Tory ought to have a tenpenny nail driven through his ———— head on a platform. Again, if the Charter was not granted on the 6th May, he Edwards would not answer for the consequences. He had 5,000 able fellows like himself, at Blackwood, that he could call together by a blow of his hand in support of the cause, if required. He had also a sister a Chartist who was getting up a petition, and every wife in Pontypool who did not sign it ought to be sent to hell.

Vincent was now looked upon as a most dangerous character, and when he visited Newport on the 16th of April, permission to hold a meeting at the Ship and Pilot Inn was refused to him. A meeting was held however at the Bush Inn, which was subsequently adjourned to Pentonville. On the following day Vincent held another meeting, at which he was supported by Mr. Wm. Townsend, Mr. Ed. Thomas, and Mr. Thos. Turner. Vincent exhorted the people to be prepared when the moment for resistance to the government came, and concluded with these words: To your tents O Israel! and then with one voice, one heart, and one blow, Perish the privileged orders! Death to the Aristocracy!

These violent speeches, which were repeated in every populous district, produced the results naturally to be expected. In the smithies at Newport and other places in the county, great activity was visible in the manufacture of arms of various kinds, and many hawkers found it profitable to take them round the country, and even expose them for sale in the market places.

THE AUTHORITIES WAKING-UP.

It now became clear to the authorities that it was their immediate duty to prevent Vincent from further inciting the people to violence, and steps to this end were at once taken. The authorities were supported by proceedings at several great Anti-Chartist meetings held in the parish of Christchurch, where it was resolved to take measures for counteracting the consequences likely to arise from the proceedings of the Chartists, and to call the attention of the Lord Lieutenant and the Secretary of State to the sale of arms going on. At one of these meetings Mr. Harry Fry, surgeon, of Newport (who had married Mr. John Frost's second daughter, Sarah), was present, and seconded a resolution. The magistrates also held a meeting to consider what steps were necessary to preserve the peace of the town.

Vincent, on being made acquainted with these proceedings, became more outrageously violent. He attended a meeting at Pontypool on the 26th April, when he stated to those present that their meeting had been declared illegal by drivelling idiots—contemptible, insidious knaves. A proclamation had been issued, and they were bound to arrest him; and he demanded to be arrested.

Efforts were now put forth in many parts of the county, and in various ways, to counteract the influence of the Chartist agitation. Anti-Chartist meetings were held, but these seemed to have no effect in withdrawing the men from the movement. At a meeting held Coalbrook Vale, April 29th, at which Mr. Crawshay Bailey presided, Mr. James Brown addressed the gathering with much earnestness, and described Zephaniah Williams, one of the Chartist leaders, as one who believed there was no God, no Eternity, and had no belief in future rewards and punishments. Ministers of religion interposed, and the Rev. J. Francis, Vicar of St. Paul's, Newport, preached a special sermon to the Chartists, at which Vincent and other leaders were present. The preacher was listened to with attention, but no apparent good resulted. The Chartist leaders still held meetings, and continued their agitation. On May 1st a meeting of Chartists at Tredegar was attended by Jones, of Pontypool, and Edwards, the mad baker, of Newport. On the following day another meeting was held at Risca. The authorities now resolved to adopt more potent measures than they had done, and accordingly, on a report from Monmouth, Lord John Russell ordered to Newport a detachment of military force, comprising 105 rank and file with officers, of the 29th Regiment. This force was strengthened by the formation at Christchurch, early in May, of a Corps of Yeomanry, called the West Monmouthshire Yeomanry ; and it was further resolved, in public meeting, to swear in special constables. Six members of the London Police Force were sent down to properly organize these constables.

APPREHENSION OF VINCENT AND OTHERS.

Vincent was arrested in London, and conveyed to Newport, where, on the 10th of May, he was, with other persons, brought before the local Justices assembled at the King's Head Hotel, and ultimately committed to Monmouth Gaol on a charge of unlawfully meeting in a riotous and seditious assembly. The imprisonment of Vincent did not stop the agitation, for other leaders continued it with increased zeal. The unusual commercial prosperity of the district, too, infused a spirit of independence among the masses of the people, rendering them less amenable to authority, and more susceptible to the poison of disaffection. Employment was plentiful, and a higher rate of wages paid than had before been known.

At most of the meetings now held, Vincent's imprisonment was a subject for much declamation. Frost referred to it at Blackwood on the 20th May, and again at Caerleon on the 23rd, when a collection for his defence was suggested. Beside agitating on behalf of the Charter, Frost conducted himself in a most obnoxious way to all who differed from him. A placard issued by him, and printed by one John Partridge, was considered calculated to incite the people to violence against the Mayor (Mr. Thomas

Phillips), upon which an application was made on June 8th in the Court of Queen's Bench for a rule to call upon Frost and Partridge to show cause why a criminal information should not be filed against them. In the face of other circumstances, the matter was allowed to pass over. The friends of Vincent continued their exertions in his behalf, and on the 25th of June, on application to Mr. Justice Patteson in London, he was released on bail, to be of good behaviour until the Assizes. These were opened on 31st July, at Monmouth, the Judges being Baron Alderson and Justice Williams. The Chartist prisoners were—Henry Vincent, 26; William Anselm Townsend, 24; William Edwards, 42; and John Dickenson, 57. They were all found guilty of attending illegal meetings, and Vincent and Edwards of having used seditious and violent language. The sentences of imprisonment passed were— Vincent 1 year, Edwards 9 months, and Townsend and Dickenson 6 months each. An indictment against Frost was traversed to next Assizes.

In the evidence given considerable light was thrown upon the danger which existed to society from the movement in which the prisoners were concerned. One witness, named Joseph Johnson, deposed that Townsend had spoken to him about ordering "from 200 to 300 muskets, 500 or 600 cutlasses, and pistols in proportion;" and Mr. Needham, manager of the Varteg Iron Works, deposed that so permeated were the people of the district with Chartist doctrines that, when in April special constables were sworn in, he could not get a single man to serve.

After these convictions, matters quieted down. Ministers of religion continued their efforts to dissuade the people from their folly, and for a time there was a little diversion. On Sunday, August 11th, a body of 230 or 240 Chartists attended Divine Service at St. Woolos Church, and again in the evening they were present at Hope Chapel. Meetings of Chartists continued to be held, but there was less violence of language, and the immediate object sought by them was the release of Vincent. At the meetings on the Hills, there was talk about securing the "Sacred Month," understood to be a month during which there should be an entire suspension of work. Mr. Frost more than once expressed his disapproval of the movement.

THE CRISIS APPROACHING.

It was known that meetings of the lodges throughout the county were frequently held, at which the members contributed money for certain purposes; but it was not until November had set in that the authorities had any information that a formidable rising was contemplated. There seems to have been at least two Chartist Lodges in Newport, one being held at the Old Bush Inn, Commercial Street (kept by a Mr. Evans), and another at the Royal Oak, in Thomas Street. Meetings were also held at the Prince of Wales Inn, Cardiff Road. The principal lodge, however, and that

CHARTIST RIOTS.

at which the attack upon Newport is said to have been planned and matured, was held at a public-house called the Coach and Horses, at Blackwood. Here, probably from its central position in the county, Frost frequently met the other leaders of the party, and consulted with them as to their lawless projects.

The outline of the great movement was this: The members of the various lodges throughout the county were to assemble, fully armed, on the evening of Sunday, the 3rd of November, and then march towards Newport. The men were to march in three divisions: one starting from Blackwood, under the command of Frost; a second, comprising the men collected from Brynmawr and Ebbw Vale, were to leave the latter place, commanded by Zephaniah Williams; and the third division, comprising the contingent from Blaenavon, Abersychan, and intermediate places, was arranged to leave Pontypool, headed by William Jones. These three divisions were directed to meet at midnight, at the Cefn—about two miles from Newport—and from thence march into the town, where it was expected they would be able to arrive about two o'clock. The leaders contemplated that the inhabitants would be asleep, entertaining no suspicion of danger. The troops were then to be attacked, the bridge across the Usk broken down, the passage of the Mail stopped, and possession of the town gained. The non-arrival of the Mail at Birmingham was there to be taken as a signal of the success of the rising in Monmouthshire, and the insurrectionary movement was then to be extended throughout the kingdom.

How this daring scheme failed, and what a miserable *fiasco* the whole affair proved, the following particulars will fully show:—

GATHERING OF FORCES.

Frost had been busy during the week preceding the Riot in meeting Williams, Jones, and other delegates, and concerting with them the measures concerning their great uprising. On Friday, November 1st, Frost, Williams, and Jones, with about thirty other delegates, met at the Coach and Horses, Blackwood, when a return of the number of armed men that could be mustered was made, and the final arrangements determined upon. On Saturday night, meetings of all the lodges in the district were held, and fully attended. The members paid up their contributions and levies, and arrangements were made to put them all under command. Most of them knew from prior circumstances that some momentous movement was about to be made, and the excitement among them was intense.

Some idea of their organization may be gathered from a paper produced at one of the magisterial examinations, and of which the following is a copy:—" Let us form into sections, by choosing a good staunch independent brother at the head of each section; that is to say each section to be composed of ten men, who are known to him to be sincere, so that the head of each section may know his men. Thus five sections will comprise 56 men and officers. Then these five officers—such as corporals—will choose a head officer, so that he may give his five officers notice ; so these 50 men are to be called a bye-name ; then three fifties will compose a company, and the three officers will choose a proper person to command the 155 in a company, officers and all, such as a captain. Then three companies will compose 495 men and officers, which officer will be such as a brigade-general. So three brigades will choose a chief, which will be 1,485 men and officers, which chief officer is to be in the style of a conventional-general. So that by these means the signal 'W.R.' can be given in two hours' notice, within seven miles, by the head officer noticing every officer under him, until it comes to the deacons or corporals to notice their ten men ; the officers to have bye-names—not military names."

The scheme was made known that the forces were to proceed to Newport, stop the Mail coaches and the traffic, and then occupy and guard the town. At one of the lodge meetings, when the men were urged to bring arms when they next assembled, one of the members reminded his hearers that they had proposed to hold their meetings peaceably throughout the country, but instead of doing so they were now carrying arms, which was against the law. "Yes ;" the leaders urged, "but if we do not break the old law, we shall never get a new." On Sunday all was completed, and Frost, at headquarters, was engaged in issuing directions for the assembly of his forces together, and arranging the order of the march. While doing this, he was continually receiving information from other quarters.

SCENE AT BLACKWOOD.

The village and neighbourhood of Blackwood was in a state of unwonted excitement. Chartists were pouring into the place by every road—some noisy and full of bravado ; others with a dogged determination pictured in their countenances. Men of all ages were there—fathers and sons, heads of families, and those who were strangers in the land. As darkness drew on, the numbers increased, and the sight was one altogether unprecedented. Never in the times of the feudal contests had a more promiscuous gathering taken place to drive back an invading enemy than was now assembled to carry terror through the district and to the town of Newport.

From Tredegar and Sirhowy they came in hundreds, displaying in their hands the results of weeks, aye months, of long and secret labour. In the recesses of the mountain side—far from the ordinary path of human beings—forges had been put up, and many men had set themselves to the manufacture of formidable pikes and other weapons, and to the casting of bullets in large numbers. To-night the forges were silent ; black darkness reigned where glowing fires had been frequent for some time past ; and the products of their labour were to be utilised for the cause. Rain had been falling during the greater part of the day; shower succeeded shower with scarcely a period of intermission. The mountain-tops were enveloped in rain-clouds, the wind blew in strong gusts, and there appeared every probability that the night would continue both wet and boisterous. Still, the condition of the weather seemed to have no dispiriting effect upon the crowds assembled. By instructions previously given, every man brought the best weapon of defence and attack that he could command. Many bore firearms, some swords, others mandrils, bill-hooks, pikes, or spears. The peacefully-disposed inhabitants were struck with terror, and hid themselves in the recesses of their dwellings, and few persons were visible but those actually engaged in the wicked design.

At Bargoed a similar state of things existed. A large meeting was held on Saturday night, and again on Sunday morning. The chapel services were deserted, and assemblies took place outside, instead of inside, the chapel walls. In the morning as the men met together, they were instructed to meet at six in the evening; and at six, when they again met, they were ordered to meet at a later hour, and to provide for the journey to Newport. Here, as in other places, houses were searched; and where men were found or known to be, they were dragged from bed by force (if unwilling) from their wives and families. It was stated that such was the tyranny exercised by the desperadoes, that one party absolutely murdered in cold blood two unfortunate men who refused to follow them.

The centre of all action was a room at the Coach and Horses, Blackwood, where sat John Frost as a commander-in-chief, issuing his orders and receiving reports from his subordinates. About seven o'clock a messenger, conspicuous in a glazed hat, made his appearance, and straightway reported himself to Mr. Frost. The purport of the intelligence brought by him speedily became known, and created great interest. He told the people that he had just come from Newport; that "the soldiers there were in the Barracks; that they were all Chartists; that their arms and ammunition were all packed; and that they were all ready to come up on the Hills, only they were waiting for the Chartists to go down to fetch them." The enthusiasm became intensified; and Frost, taking advantage of the moment, came out of the house and addressed his followers. He wore a rough big coat, and round his neck was wrapped a large red cravat. In brief but encouraging terms, he told them their enemies were flying in all directions, and that it was time for them to be off. Did any of them want ammunition? The Cefn was to be their rendezvous, where they were to meet Zephaniah Williams with 5,000 brethren; and William Jones, of Pontypool, with 2,000 more.—A man named Davies, in a few homely expressions, endeavoured still further to excite the ardour of the men assembled, urging them to "go on," as they were enough to eat Newport. Arrangements were made for an immediate start. A password was quickly circulated, that every man might be able to distinguish friend from foe. "Beans" was the word, and "well" the challenge— the whole word being "Beanswell," the name of a well-known locality in Newport. When they met a stranger they were to use the word "Beans," and if he replied "Well," they would know that he was engaged in the same object. If the stranger could not give the answer, he was to be made a prisoner. Before starting, a suggestion was made to scour the village, with a view to bring forth any inhabitants who refrained from joining the mad movement. There was an evident division in the camp upon the point. Some were in favour of it, and proceeded to perform the operation. In one instance a division of the mob—about fifty persons—forcibly separated a man from his wife as they were proceeding on the turnpike road towards their dwelling, and compelled the former to swell the ranks of the deluded criminals. The majority, however, dwelt only upon the greater enterprise, and were impatient of delay. Frost, like a skilful general, secured a moment's attention, placed himself at the head of the gathering, and lustily bawled out the command, "Follow me!" He was readily obeyed; but obedience was not order, and to infuse discipline among such an heterogeneous mass proved an utter failure. Some of the *aide-de-camps* urged the men to form ranks, and went so far as to place them in threes and fours; but, in many instances, the interference was gruffly resented, and they were told to "mind their own business, and let everybody do as they liked." So they went forward in higgledy-piggledy disorder. It soon became evident that some of the men had no heart in the proceeding, and these endeavoured to drop behind. Such faint hearts very speedily discovered that the contingency had been anticipated, and armed officers were in the rear to guard and keep up the laggards who came under their notice.

ZEPHANIAH WILLIAMS AT NANTYGLO.

Leaving Frost and his party now journeying onwards towards the rendezvous, a glance may be taken at what was passing this Sunday evening higher up among "the Hills." At Nantyglo the usual quietude of the Sabbath was rudely disturbed by the movements of the Chartists. From an early hour in the day the Royal Oak (kept by Zephaniah Williams) was largely frequented by them, and rumours were prevalent that their intentions were of the most sinister character. The peaceable inhabitants were much alarmed, and knew not whether it were wise to remain at home or fly to other parts, leaving their property without protection. As the Chartists during the day gathered strength, detachments pressed into their ranks, with oaths and violence, all persons who came across their path. On meeting a man, they proceeded somewhat after the following summary fashion :—"Where are you going?" was the first question with which they accosted him. "Home," or "Nowhere, particular" would probably be the reply, upon which, with the utterance of language not lightly repeated, they directed him to join the body, or threatened to run him through with a spear or pike if he made any demur. The touch of a piece of pointed steel was generally sufficient to silence remonstrance, and one more was added to the ranks. During the day several apparent strangers were seen in conference with Williams; and orders were circulated among the men that they were to meet on the mountain in the evening, and bring bread and cheese with them, as probably they would want victuals before they returned to their homes, an intimation at the same time being conveyed that if they neglected to attend their lives would be in danger. A very indefinite idea prevailed as to what was to be done on the mountain; but it was generally understood that some great movement had been determined upon by the leaders, the purport of which would be disclosed at the meeting. It was expected that about 4,000 persons would attend. Before leaving the Royal Oak, all the men who had not obtained arms or weapons from other sources were duly supplied with them in the lodge-room. Guns and swords were not numerous, but pikes, forged for the purpose, were plentiful. When these were exhausted, dangerous weapons were improvised by fastening knives at the end of sticks. Some of the men were furnished with a simple mopstick, and told to defend themselves with that as best they could. It was hinted as not improbable that some persons would attend to interrupt the meeting, and in that case the arms would prove of some service; but there was to be no shedding of blood, nor anything of that sort. The place of meeting on the mountain was between Nantyglo and Ebbw Vale, at a great height above the surrounding villages. Here they began to assemble soon after five o'clock; and ere darkness covered the scene, the misguided men were to be seen in droves upon every high road and bye-path, flocking towards the meeting-place, until between four and five thousand assembled, nearly every one armed with such weapons as he had been able to procure. The spot selected was one where a large assembly might conveniently be addressed. There was a "tump" at this part of the mountain, and upon this "tump," where he might be seen and heard by all around, Zephaniah Williams mounted to address his followers. The record of his oration is brief; but it was not a time for many words. They were called upon to act. He said: "My dear Chartists, you need not be frightened, because we are bound to be in Newport by two o'clock. The soldiers will not touch you." At the mere mention of the word "soldiers," the assembly uplifted their arms, and gave one long, wild shout or war-whoop, which seemed to stir the elements and make the dim mountain reverberate with the sound. "We don't care for them" was echoed again and again; and after a few fiery observations in Welsh, and the exclamation, "Come on, boys!" Zephaniah Williams stepped down from his rostrum, and, placing himself at the head of the party, led the march. This onward movement.

was hailed by the majority of the large assembly as a great relief. For two hours they had been exposed on the bleak mountain-side to the incessant pelting of the pitiless storm. Drenched to the skin they were with rain, and chilled with the keen blast of the merciless wind. Such a trial tested the strength of their convictions, and if credit be due to them in any respect, it surely is for their tenacity of purpose under such adverse circumstances. Ere they had gained the tramway at the foot of the mountain at Blaina, where a slight halt was first made to gather up the forces, the design disclosed to them on the height had been freely discussed; and Zephaniah Williams, as the leader, had more than once to give replies to very pointed and pertinent questions put by some of his followers. "What did they want," enquired one, "down to Newport? Were they going to be killed all?" "No," said Williams, "I hope that we shall come safe back. Nobody will be killed there." Satisfying his querists, and sustaining their courage to the best of his ability, they pursued their way down the tramroad towards Risca.

JONES AT ABERSYCHAN.

While the events recorded in the preceding narrative were transpiring, William Jones and his supporters were no less active in the district of which Abersychan was the centre. Soon after daylight on Sunday morning, Jones was abroad, mounted on a horse provided for him, urging his lieutenants to get the people together not later than 2 p.m., with a view to an aggregate muster at the Race at a later period of the day.

Large crowds assembled, but still many absentees were noted, and, accordingly, a series of domiciliary visits were paid in search of men supposed to be breaking faith with their brethren in not appearing at the trysting-place. Men, after labouring all day, found, on their return home, a number of Chartists awaiting their arrival, and compelling them to go with them; even refusing to grant a few minutes' delay for the purpose of refreshment. On the same evening a large meeting was held at Jones's residence—the Bristol Beerhouse, Pontypool—and, according to instructions, the men came armed with guns, pikes, and such other weapons as they had in their possession, or could lay their hands upon. The rooms of the house, both upstairs and downstairs, were crowded with excited men. A man of influence—one Shellard—was busy in seeing that men were furnished with weapons. Guns, pistols, and trusty staves were here exhibited; and, after a supply had been made to the many who required them, Shellard urged them to leave the house for the meeting at the Race, or they would be late. He directed those who had no weapons to go to a house at the top of Trosnant, where they would find guns, swords, and pistols. They were to take which they thought would be of service to them, and the man in charge would not say a word to them. Such a simple proceeding was not fully comprehended by all Jones's associates, for it is recorded that a collier, having received these directions, replied, "Damn you, do you think I am going to rob the man's house? You may do it yourself."

At ten o'clock there was a goodly meeting as regards numbers, but the proceedings were brief. The weather was terrific, and Jones found his energies severely taxed in his efforts to keep the courage of the men to the sticking-point. He explained that the people of Newport were expecting their arrival in three bodies, and the necessity there was for being prompt in their engagements.

At Pontnewynydd the contingent was with difficulty collected together, the rendezvous being a beerhouse kept by Mr. John Llewellyn. When the muster was nearly complete, they started to join Jones at the Race, and arrived just in time to receive Jones's final commands. There were many who no doubt had attended the meeting from no other motive than curiosity, and at its termination were desirous of finding their way home again. Their desire, however, was not easily accomplished, as armed men were stationed at various points to prevent the escape of those who were disposed to desert from their comrades.

Jones's orders were that they should march towards Newport, and on the road towards that town they speedily began to make their way. The men carrying spears were directed to go first, and those who bore firearms next, the rear being composed of the "irregulars." In this order they marched about five abreast. Having started from Abersychan, they broke into many houses on the road, forcing the inmates to join their ranks.

During the whole night, Chartists had continued to pass through Pontypool, some in straggling parties, and then in larger numbers. About three o'clock Superintendent Roberts and her constables went into the middle of a large party and captured a big ruffianly fellow, who carried a pike measuring seven feet in the handle. About five o'clock the main body of the Chartists passed through the town, and hesitated for ten minutes before the Station-house whether or not to attack it, and release the prisoners. They, however, passed on, and arrived at the New Inn, Croes-y-Ceilog, about eleven o'clock. The knowledge of a public-house being at this place was irresistible. Men, hungry and already wearied by exposure to the bitter weather, rushed in for shelter and refreshment, and, so far as they were able, disposed themselves for rest and comfort.

At this place (Croes-y-Ceilog) a noteworthy incident occurred which will well serve to illustrate the unlawful and wicked proceedings of these misguided men. The persons concerned were two gentlemen of Pontypool, namely, Mr. Barnabas Brough, a brewer and wine merchant, and Mr. Thomas Watkins, a currier. Mr. Brough's statement is so clear and circumstantial that the reader will best be informed by quoting as nearly as possible Mr. Brough's own narrative. He stated :—" I was at Newport on Sunday, the

3rd November, and left at nine o'clock, with a view to return home, in a horse and gig. Mr. Thomas Watkins was with me. We got as far as Croes-y-Ceilog, when the horse became knocked up, and we determined to walk to Pontypool. It was excessively wet and dark. About half-a-mile after we started, we were met by an armed force. We were ordered to 'stand' by the party, who made us prisoners. The man who was at the head of the party appeared to be the leader. Our names were asked, and they were correctly informed. The person interrogating us then said that we must turn round, and go with them. I said I would rather not. They were going towards Newport. They said if we went quietly, we should be taken care of. I remonstrated against this interference with my liberty, when I was told to hold my tongue, or it would be worse for me. I wanted to know by what right they interfered with my liberty, and I was again told to hold my tongue, and turn round and walk with them, which I did. Immediately on so doing, two men were ordered to guard us in front, and two behind, with pikes. The leader had what appeared to me to be a gun. He marched at my left. In this order we went towards Newport. There appeared to me to be about forty or fifty in the first group, but it was too dark to correctly distinguish the number. I did not attempt to escape; but just before we got to the Marshes Gate, I asked permission to cross the hedge, which I thought they would accede to. I leaped the hedge, and fell into three or four feet of water. Several voices called out to me, and threatened to blow my brains out immediately. I felt the guns near me, and I fancied I saw three. I begged them not to fire, and promising them to return, they allowed me to do so. We went then to a shed or cowhouse immediately facing the Toll House, which we found crowded with armed men. After some remonstrance, we were taken to the Toll House. Here I borrowed a pair of stockings of the Toll House-keeper, and changed them, being guarded all the time by a man with a drawn sword. After some time we were taken upstairs, where I fell asleep. Subsequently we were ordered down again; and, still guarded, we were taken across the canal, and up the lane leading to Risca. During the time we were passing along this lane I observed signal rockets being fired between Newport and Risca. We arrived at the Cefn about half-past three or four o'clock. From the Cefn we went to the Welsh Oak, and whilst there Mr. Frost came in. An explanation of the circumstances was made, and Mr. Frost stated that I was an old acquaintance of his, and that, although he detested my politics, he had great respect for me."

Both Mr. Brough and his companion, Mr. Watkins, were immediately liberated.

While the two gentlemen named and their guards had been moving rapidly across the country to meet Mr. Frost, Jones and the main body of his followers remained still hanging about the precincts of Croes-y-Ceilog searching from house to house, and compelling, by threats and force, every man they encountered to go with them. The inhabitants of the district were in consequence placed in a state of the greatest fear. It was five o'clock on Monday morning ere a further start was made. Jones then gave his lieutenant a sword and a dagger, and despatched him on the road with the bulk of his followers, remaining himself to gather together the stragglers hanging behind. He found a number lurking in corners and behind screens, pretending to be larking, but all ineffectually endeavouring to escape from their companions. Jones was equal to the occasion, and, presenting a pistol at their heads, with a threat to blow out their brains if they continued larking, succeeded in getting them to leave without further delay.

Pursuing the road towards Newport, the main body of Jones's division, still numbering between 2,000 and 3,000 men, arrived at the Green House, Llantarnam (a noted roadside Alehouse), and here another halt was made. The alarm which the Chartists created soon spread, and Mr. Blewitt, the Member of the Monmouth Boroughs, who resided at Llantarnam Abbey, heard of their approach. He immediately went into the main road to meet them, and found a very imposing assembly of armed men, and heard that they had been impressing into their ranks, and offering violence to people whom they met. He addressed the misguided men for some time, and represented that certain ruin awaited them if they set themselves against the authorities of the country. His remarks made some impression upon his hearers, but the more active efforts of the leaders prevailed, and they marched onward towards Newport. Soon the leading body came to Malpas Court, where they amused themselves by another little diversion. About 150 of them entered the stable yard of the Court, and seizing the gardener and coachman, compelled them to leave their duties and follow in the rear. On arriving at the Marshes Turnpike Gate, at a short distance from Newport, several persons were stationed their, and directed the body of the people to turn up the lane (now known as the Barrack Hill) towards Penylan. Here they were expecting to meet or to hear some tidings of the other divisions, which Jones knew to be marching towards Newport upon the same errand as himself and followers.

FURTHER PROGRESS OF JOHN FROST.

It may be advisable at this point to follow up the progress of Frost, who, with his party, we have already traced making his way along the tramroad. After calling at various public-houses, and passing through Newbridge, the mob reached Risca, where the same lawlessness prevailed. House after house was visited and searched. In most cases the men, fearing to be impressed, had left the houses and secreted themselves in the neighbouring woods, or at a distance from the roadside; and the women, left by themselves or in the care of children, were half dead with fear, screaming, and swooning.

Such a state of things created a very great inclination in the minds of many to put an end to the matter by turning back; but the bolder spirits overcame the scruples of the more tender-hearted, and further progress was made.

Most of the leaders were on horseback, and carried lanterns, and were riding to and fro.

The party, about four o'clock in the morning, approached the roadside inn called the Welsh Oak (kept by Henry Charles), about four miles from Newport. The Chartists began to arrive between ten and eleven o'clock, and at length filled the house to overflowing. The resources of this small hostelry were altogether insufficient for the demand of such a large and devouring rabble; and it appeared an impossibility for one-tenth of the number to have the smallest taste of beer if they remained; so many made a virtue of necessity, and proceeded further on to a public-house at the Cefn.

At the two places named there was a lengthy halt, and the men sought shelter in all the houses of the neighbourhood. There had been ominous rumours throughout the preceding day as to what was contemplated, and soon after midnight, when the van or skirmishers of the Chartist force made their appearance, the whole district was on the *qui vive*. Neighbours called upon neighbours, and afforded each other the latest information and best protection they were able. The experience of Thomas Saunders, a farmer residing near the Welsh Oak, is not uninteresting. He heard a noise on the tramway near his house, about midnight, after he had retired to bed, but, thinking it was some people at the public-house, he lay down again. In a few minutes, hearing some one calling him by name, he went to the window of his bedroom, and asked, "What do you want at this time of night?" "Rise in a minute, and then I will tell you," was the response. Saunders got up, and then his friend said, "Now you had better move off, because there are hundreds and thousands of Chartists on the tramroad." Such an alarming statement caused Saunders at once to rush off and hide himself in his barn among the straw. His thoughts of safety in seclusion were very soon, however, rudely dispelled, as before long a troop of Chartists came to the barn, opened the door, and made an entry. He ascertained from their conversation that their chief object was shelter from the rain, and, finding them none other than peaceably disposed, thought it unwise to resist them. Saunders's thoughts naturally reverted to his dwelling-house, and, creeping out of the barn, made his way home, when he found the house full of Chartists, taking their ease before a good fire which they had made. Saunders's fears made him very uneasy, for no sooner did he satisfy himself that the house was not destroyed, than he was seized with a dread that the men would set his barn on fire; so he proceeded thither to caution them not to be careless with the candles, and again returned to his house. Many of the men availed themselves of the good fire to dry their clothes.

Frost was now anxiously looking out for communications from the other leaders, and urging them to send on their forces with all speed. He was uneasy at the unexpected delay which he had experienced in his progress. It was getting daylight, and he nervously paraded up and down the road with his hands in his pockets. Men, who during the night had made fruitless enquiries for him, discovered him now, and he was again and again interrogated by some of the pitiable half-drunken creatures under his influence. Some of them thought the march they had undergone quite enough for them, and that they had better return to their homes. Frost, however, was of different opinion. He told the men that they had better not return, and entered into details as to what would be further required of them. They were to proceed to Newport, where they were to attack the new Poor House, and take the soldiers and their arms. Then he would direct them to a Store House where there was plenty of powder. They were next to blow up the Bridge, and stop the Welsh Mail which ran to the North. That would be tidings to those in expectation of what was being done; and they would commence in the North a similar movement on Monday night. He further sarcastically remarked that when he reached Newport he should be able to see two or three of his friends or enemies there. While these statements and disclosures much excited many of the mob, there were others —and those the most sober among them—whom it affected in a different way. They contemplated with fear the lawlessness as well as the danger of the proceeding; and many made unceasing efforts to escape by hiding behind bushes, and secreting themselves in sheds and other places. Very few succeeded, however, and those detected in their attempts were threatened with the most summary vengeance by having pikes thrust through them or their brains blown out by firearms.

During this lengthy halt those who had guns were ordered to prove them, in order that they might discover whether they had not been rendered unserviceable by the continuous rain. This process was again ordered to be repeated farther on the road at Pye Corner and in Tredegar Park.

LAWLESSNESS OF WILLIAMS'S FORCE.

During the stay which Frost and his companions made at the Welsh Oak, Zephaniah Williams had been urging on the rear of his men to the best of his ability; but the tempestuous weather was much against rapidity of movement, and the desire for plunder was strong among many. House after house on the road was broken into, and the inmates summoned either to follow in the ranks or to give up any arms they might possess. Every public-house on the road was literally besieged, and great difficulty was experienced in getting the men, after they had been supplied with refreshment, to depart, in order to make room for others. The refreshments obtained were in most cases paid for by the captains, and not by the men themselves. At the Coach and

Horses, Llanhilleth (fifteen miles from Newport), the landlord was aroused from his slumbers soon after eleven o'clock, and found a dozen men at the door, demanding refreshment. He came downstairs, and, having satisfied their requirements, they departed, and the Boniface returned to his bed. In a few minutes, however, a still more urgent demand was made from another party; and upon the landlord opening the door a perfect rush was made into the house, almost bereaving the landlord of his wits. About half-past one o'clock, on Monday morning, Williams, driving up the rear, reached the house. His force had all then gone forward, and, dripping with wet, he sat down by the fire and drank a pint of beer.

Williams made some enquiry about a horse, as he was anxious to get on faster, fearing that the delay would lead to serious inconvenience. The landlord possessed five horses in his stable on the opposite side of the way; but, trembling for their safety (as his late visitors had stolen various things which they could lay their hands upon), told some delusive statement about their being two miles up the valley. In the end, however, he arranged to afford Williams assistance, and called up his servant to prepare a horse and tram for his use. As soon as the tram was ready, Williams and a few friends got in, and they were driven off down the road as far as Tyn-y-Cwm, where they arrived about seven o'clock, and where Williams got out.

Williams's party, without a commander, seemed to increase in lawlessness as they proceeded. Nearly every house on their way was visited. The doors were burst open, the windows smashed, and the inmates dragged out of bed, and compelled to go along with the mob. It was natural that persons so impressed should make every effort to escape, but woe betide the unlucky creature if detected in the attempt.

An incident of this kind occurred at Abercarn to a person named George Lloyd, who, when proceeding to his home at Blaina, had been arrested by the mob, and forced to walk with them. He several times tried to escape on the road, but, being detected, they placed a guard over him, who amused themselves by pushing him along and poking him in the back with a stick, swearing that they would serve him out. On arriving at Abercarn they had to pass by the canal, and here they threw the poor fellow into the water. After much struggling he succeeded in getting out; but his tormentors still pursued their cruelty, until, exhausted by cold, wet, and hunger, Lloyd fell down by the roadside insensible. Here they left him, and passed on. After a time he managed to creep to a neighbouring house, and, rousing the inmates, asked them to take him in. They did so, and sheltered him until six o'clock in the morning, when, believing the road to be clear, he started on his way home. About half-a-mile from Abercarn, however, at a point where the road turns off to Blaina, he fell in with a band of forty or fifty men, armed with pikes, and who were proceeding to Newport. They quickly ascertained from Lloyd his night's adventures, and made him turn round and march again towards Newport.

As another instance of lawlessness, we may mention that they made an attack upon a house about half-past one in the morning, compelling the man, under threats that they would blow up his house, to come down to open the door, giving him no time to put on his clothes. They seemed to know that there were arms in the house, and consequently, as soon as the door was opened, they walked straight into his kitchen and took two guns. On searching the other rooms they found another gun, hid behind the parlour-door, and this they also took, together with a pistol and bayonet, shot belt, a pouch, and about half a pound of powder.

On arriving at Newbridge, enquiries were repeated as to where they were going, and for what purpose ; but the only information vouchsafed was that they were going to Newport with Mr. Frost, whom they would meet at Cefn de Machog.

At the Welsh Oak Williams came up with Frost, and both then made an attempt to again get their followers into something like order. Williams went round to the houses rousing the men from their shelter, and in most cases kindly entreating the men to proceed. At Farmer Saunders's he found the house full, and upon his saying, "Come, my men, let's go," the men made themselves ready as soon as they could, and off they started about 7 a.m. Williams was not slow in detecting those who were apparently hanging back, and commanding them to go on with the others. He directed them to fall in two-and-two.

The numbers being now considerably augmented by the successive arrivals of Williams's detachments, a further advance was decided upon. Frost commanded those who carried guns to take the front, those who had pikes were to go next, and to be followed by the men armed with bludgeons. Those who had no arms were to follow behind. Other dispositions of the men were made, rendering it evident that he contemplated serious work. It had rained incessantly during the night, and the fear that the guns would be rendered useless by damp powder led those who carried them to try their efficiency. Reports were frequent, and alarming to those not participating in the enterprise : even to those who were, the sound of the guns had a different and contrary effect. It stimulated the ardour of some, while the temerity of others, who contemplated that some people would be killed, was turned to cowardice or remorse. There were some who had spirit enough to remonstrate with Frost upon his proceedings, and amongst them was a man named Hodge, who upon hearing these commands given went up and said to Frost, "In the name of God what are you doing ; are you going to attack any place or people?" Frost declared his intentions more fully than before, which were to attack Newport and take it, to blow up the bridge and stop the Welsh mail from proceeding to Birmingham. He further said that there would be three delegates waiting for the mail at Birmingham, and if they found it did not arrive, the attack would commence in Birmingham and continue further to the north of England and Scotland. The delay of the mail was to be the signal to the whole nation. Hodge urged that he might as well lead the men to a slaughter-house to be slaughtered, and with warmth told Frost that he imitated a butcher leading a flock of lambs to the slaughter-house. He begged Frost to desire the men to return to the hills. Frost's reply was brief but scornfully sarcastic. His only words were, "Do you think so?" and turned away to control the mutinous spirit which he feared might probably spread. From this point desertions from the ranks were numerous, though comparatively few compared with the immense number marching upon Newport under these unusual circumstances. Hodge jumped over a hedge, and, having remained hid for some time among briars and brambles, allowed the mob to pass on, and then ran away home as fast as he could. Frost, as before, took the lead, and Williams remained in the rear. When the men were fairly started again on the road, Williams ran back to Farmer Saunders, and asked if he might dry himself, as he was very wet. Permission was only too readily given; and while standing at this farmhouse fire, the following colloquy is recorded to have taken place:—

Saunders: Mr. Williams, where are you going?
Williams: Why do you ask?
Saunders: Because some of the men in my house this morning told me you were going to Monmouth to draw Vincent out of prison.
Williams: No, we don't attempt that. We are going to give a turn as far as Newport.

While Williams and a few friends were thus enjoying the comforts of a cheerful fire, detachments of the mob were scouring the roads, ransacking the dwelling houses, and continuing the practice of violence to all men with whom they came into contact. At Tydee a man named Joseph Anthony was discovered at his stable avocations just after daybreak, between six and seven o'clock, and compelled against his will to leave his work. On his refusing to accompany them, the armed men threatened him, and guarded him until after they had passed through Tredegar Park and came to Courtybella, where he managed to effect his escape.

PREPARATIONS AT NEWPORT.

We have followed the movements of Frost and his followers from their head quarters at Blackwood as far as Courtybella, ready to enter the town of Newport. We have traced Zephaniah Williams from the gathering together of his forces at Nantyglo; to their amalgamation with the forces of John Frost, and we have further also described the march of the third division under William Jones from Abersychan district to within a short distance of Newport, and waiting an opportunity to effect a junction with the other divisions.

CHARTIST RIOTS.

We now turn to describe the action of those responsible for the protection and safety of life and property in the district.

It was generally believed by the inhabitants of Pontypool from rumours in circulation that the plans of the Chartists were to send forward a contingent of their forces to Newport, and those who were left behind were to attack the Station house, and the squire's house; sieze all the arms and take the Lord Lieutenant prisoner. In this belief the authorities called out the pensioners and special constables the former being armed each with a firelock and bayonet, and the special constables with their own single and double barrel guns. The force altogether numbered about 80, this including a corporal's party of the gallant 45th and the servants and dependents of the Lord Lieutenant. These were divided, one half being located at the Station house, and the other half at the Mansion, with arrangements to co-operate together if necessary.

Abergavenny was in a state of intense excitement for several days, as a rumour had been circulated that a large body of the Chartists intended to march into the town from the Hills. One company of the Scots Greys, who were stationed in Abergavenny, went along Brecon road to Crickhowell and around by Glasyln, and another company proceeded along Merthyr road, and both companies met at Gilwern. The wildest and most absurd reports were believed, and some of the simple-minded folk expected almost every moment that the place would be nothing less than pillaged, and perhaps burnt, and the inhabitants ruthlessly slaughtered. Every man, who was willing, was sworn in as special constable, and armed with a constable's staff, which was really a rough stick or cudgel, and with the presence of so formidable a force backed by the cavalry, a feeling of security was established. Then the intelligence arrived from an authentic source that the rioters had gone in several large bodies by Nantyglo and Blaina, and Ebbw Vale and by the other ways intending to meet near Crumlin, and march into Newport.

With regard to Newport we have the advantage of referring to statement in writing originally made by Sir Thomas Phillips. the Mayor of Newport, for the purposes of the prosecution which followed the events here narrated. From this it would appear that his worship had on the 31st October, a communication from the late Samuel Homfray, Esq., then of Tredegar Iron Works, that the Chartists, who had frequent meetings in that neighbourhood, meditated violence of some kind. In the course of the evening of the same day he ascertained from a master carpenter, living at Newport, but whose name is not preserved, that the Newport Chartists met twice a week; that they had become more violent in their language, and their proceedings had given rise to a belief that some desperate proceeding would soon take place. The following day was Friday, the 1st November, and the town was more than usually excited, and the Mayor busily engaged owing to the annual municipal elections which took place. The general feeling which prevailed induced the Mayor on Saturday morning to communicate

CHARTIST RIOTS.

his suspicions to Captain Stack, the officer in command of the detachment of the 45th Regiment stationed at Newport, and suggested to him that it might be necessary to secure his detachment from surprise in case any attack should be made upon the quarters in which they were stationed. As the 5th November was approaching—always a scene of much riot and confusion in Newport—his worship thinking it possible that mischeivous men, either living in the town or introduced from a distance might take advantage of that riot and confusion to set fire to property or do other mischief, directed the Superintendent of Police to summon 150 special constables to be on duty that evening, and requested that the military might be kept in readiness to act if required. His Worship also on the same evening communicated all the information he had received to the Lord Lieutenant of the County, Capel Hanbury Leigh, Esq. At this period the Mayor had not anticipated any organised outbreak, but on Sunday morning information came in from several quarters giving particulars of what the Chartists had been doing on the previous evening, and leading to the conclusion that there would be an immediate rising. Mr. Samuel Homfray, from Tredegar, sent a letter to the Mayor; and Mr. John Llewellyn, of Abercarn, brought him reports from Nantyglo. On receiving this information, the Mayor immediately wrote to the Home Secretary, the Lord Lieutenant of the County, the Mayor of Monmouth, the Vicar of Abergavenny, the Town Clerk of Cardiff, and acquainted them of the critical state of things. The Lord Lieutenant had previously heard of what was transpiring, and was on the road to Newport when the messenger delivered to him the letter from the Mayor. On his arrival in the town a council of war was held. The Superintendent of Police was instructed to summon the special constables for that evening instead of on the following Tuesday; and Captain Stack, at the request of the Mayor and Lord Lieutenant, despatched a corporal and four or five men in a post chaise to Pontypool. In the course of the evening Mr. Brewer and Mr. Edwards, two borough magistrates, were called in, and five hundred special constables summoned were ordered to assemble, part at the King's Head, part at the Westgate, and part at the Parrot Hotels. These were placed at the disposal of Mr. Hawkins, one of the Magistrates. The Mayor himself directing that they were to keep up communications between the Westgate and Cross Hands (? High Cross). Further information came in giving rise to the most serious apprehensions. A man named Ricketts, on his way to Newport, was overtaken at Bassalleg by two men who told him there would be terrible work in Newport during the night, and requested him to call upon the Mayor and Mr. Lewis Edwards, and tell him they ought to remove from their houses with their families. Then Mr. Stephen Iggulden, landlord of the Carpenter's Arms, told the Mayor that a person who had stopped at his house on the previous night, and supposed to be a messenger from the Chartists on the Hills to Birmingham, had taken a carriage to Monmouth, and from thence had been sent on in another carriage to Worcester; and now messenger after messenger came in, all bringing confirmation of the fact that the Chartists were actually marching upon the town in armed force.

DANGEROUS RECONNOITRING.

Messengers and scouts were now sent out in all directions to watch and report their progress, and in the performance of this task some of them experienced no little danger. About ten o'clock two men named Thomas Walker (son of Mrs. Walker, of the Parrot Inn) and Richard Webb were sent on horseback to Risca with instructions to remain there until the Chartists approached the place, and then return to Newport as fast as they could. These messengers noticed nothing unusual until they reached Rogerstone Court, about four miles from Newport. Here was the residence of a gentleman named Rigby, who had invested a considerable amount of money with a view to discover coal at Risca, but failed, and his design to erect a commodious residence at this place was never completed. The messengers here saw about two dozen men standing under a wall, but they passed on unmolested towards the Welsh Oak, where they heard above the dash of the rain and the whistling of the blast a loud uproar, and sounds of cheering and firing of guns, which appeared to come from the locality just above Risca. Upon hearing this, prudence dictated that they should return at once and report to the Mayor. They accordingly turned their horses heads homewards, and were proceeding at a good pace towards Newport when on approaching Rigby's—where they had previously passed a small party of men—an attempt was made to stay their progress by a line of men stationed across the road. The mission of Walker and Webb had probably been suspected, and now it was determined, if possible, to prevent the conveyance of the intelligence which they would be in a position to communicate. Walker, however, was not daunted; but, summoning courage, called upon his horse and galloped through his assailants. Unfortunately, he did not escape without receiving in his thigh a long flesh wound, inflicted in the brief struggle by a scythe or other sharp instrument. Webb was not wounded, but narrowly escaped the contents of a pistol discharged at him. Walker succeeded in reaching the Westgate soon after midnight, where he was assisted to dismount, and his wound attended to. The Mayor's alarm was naturally increased at the episode, and he at once despatched a request to Bristol that troops might be sent to Newport from that city. As the night advanced, it was rumoured that the Chartists of Newport were assembling on the Marshes, and, in consequence, a company of special constables were sent to ascertain the truth of the rumour. They returned in a short time, and reported that they had seen a body of men near the turnpike gate, who had made their escape. The constables produced a long pike-handle which they had captured from them. Constant patrols were now kept up between the different public buildings of the town and the Barracks; and, after midnight, many men were taken into custody with arms in their possession, some of these men being townspeople, and others of whom were colliers from the Hills. Some of these prisoners were detained at the Westgate, and others sent to the Barracks. At daybreak, Henry Williams, an ironmonger of the town, and who acted on this occasion as one of the Mayor's *aide-de-camp*, went out, and on his return reported that he had seen 400 or 500 of the Chartists at Pye Corner, making their way towards Tredegar Park. Williams went out a second time, and found the body halting at Belle Vue, and cheering lustily.

THE MILITARY CALLED OUT.

The Mayor now wrote a letter to Captain Stack, requesting that he would send to the Westgate as many men under his command as he could detach without endangering his own position at the Barracks, which had been temporarily arranged at the new Union Workhouse, Stow Hill. In a short time afterwards, Lieutenant Grey, with Sergeants Daily and Armstrong and 28 rank and file under his charge, was sent with instructions to report himself to the Mayor at the Westgate. It was a quarter after eight when the soldiers appeared in front of the Hotel, where they for a few minutes halted while Lieutenant Grey communicated with the Mayor. Their appearance increased the consternation already felt; not only in the immediate neighbourhood, but in the most distant parts of the town. The soldiers were not long before the gaze of the public, for in a few minutes Lieutenant Grey reappeared with the Mayor, and, at the request of His Worship, marched his men into the stable-yard of the Westgate, and from thence through the back of the house to the large room at the eastern wing of the building, this being in the opinion of Lieut. Grey, after a careful reconnoitre of the position, the best situation from which to act, if action were found necessary. There was a desire that no menace should appear by the sight of the soldiers, and consequently, while the windows of the room were thrown up for the purpose of ventilation, the shutters were carefully closed to any view from outside the building. The Mayor directed that the gates should be closed, and also that the front door should be shut by the constables stationed there.

THE LAST HALT BEFORE ENTERING NEWPORT.

Frost and his followers began to pass the Park machine at 7 a.m. and when they arrived at Courtybella, another short halt was made, they were here enabled for the first time to glean some idea of what was doing in the town. The news of their near approach had spread, and though the people going out to meet them were not numerous, yet from every coign of advantage were found some with unsatisfied curiosity, and heedless of danger endeavouring to see what this armed, noisy force was like. Loud cheering and boisterous hurrahs were ever and anon intermingled with the ominous firing of guns. From the shipping in the lower part of the river and the works adjacent, people left their avocations and ran across the fields to be witnesses of these extraordinary proceedings.

CHARTIST RIOTS. 37

At the time the head of the party arrived at Courtybella, Zephaniah Williams in the rear, was about passing Pye Corner, the intermediate distance of a mile and a half being covered by the ranks of the many thousands who were now closing together in marching order. A gentleman named John Nicholl Hawkins, a surgeon of Newport, who knew Williams, and saw him at this point, informed him that a number of soldiers had arrived in Newport and advised the people around him to go back; but Williams very petulantly exclaimed, "Damn the soldiers! Come on, boys, and we'll show them what colliers can do in Newport!"—at the same time putting his hand to draw a pistol, Mr. Hawkins deemed it discreet quietly to move onward.

Frost, too, had heard of the soldiers being in town; and, during this last brief halt, made enquiries respecting them, and was told that about a dozen had gone to the Westgate. The news of the soldiers being in town passed rapidly from rank to rank, and seemed to be regarded as anything but a matter of serious import; rather as a matter of levity and humour. Some amused themselves by facetiously rehearsing the part which, in all probability, they would in a short time be called upon to perform. Guns were fired, swords brandished, and hooks and pikes flourished most harmlessly menacing. "That's how I would cut it!" exclaims one bravo. "I would cut it, too," says another. "Mine is damned sharp—feel it," as he held forth the keen blade for his companion's examination. A noted character, known as Jack the Fifer, desired the informant—a person named Coles—to go and tell the soldiers that they (the Chartists) would have the Westgate for themselves bye-and-bye. A man in the ranks, on hearing the observation, exclaimed, "Yes, I want a waistcoat, for mine is d—— wet!" Coles, however, who had left his breakfast to run away and see the Chartists, was neither allowed to return to his breakfast or to deliver the message he was requested to do; but compelled, by a peremptory mandate of the leaders, to fall into the ranks.

THE MARCH INTO THE TOWN.

Frost, now finding the whole body pretty well together, gave the command, "March!" "March" was re-echoed by Jack the Fifer, and other lieutenants; and the whole force then left the tramway, and took the road leading by the Friars up to Stow Church. Thence passing onward, they pursued their way down the hill, presenting an appearance almost indescribable. Frost, in his big rough coat and red cravat, led the van, immediately followed by those who carried guns, walking four or five abreast. Next came those who possessed pikes, the rear being brought up by those who wielded mandrils, pitchforks, sticks, &c.

Captain Stack, a fine Peninsular veteran, was out with his undaunted few of the 45th, near their Barracks on Stow Hill, and stood with his son, Ensign Stack, at their head; but the mass of Chartists dared not approach, though within a few hundred yards.

On the raised footway down Stow Hill were hundreds of people, whose curiosity was greater than their fear ; and at the windows of the houses, from which a view of Stow Hill might be obtained, faces might be noticed cautiously peeping as if fearful of some disaster befalling them, if only observed. Where such faces were noticed, the guns were immediately directed thereto, causing the concealed spectator to start back with sudden terror. Men engaged on the roof of the Catholic Church, then in course of erection, hastened down in fright, and escaped from all apparent danger.

On came the Chartists at a quick pace, shouting excitedly, "Clear the road ! clear the road !" "To the Westgate !" "Our prisoners !" &c., making it evident to bystanders that the Westgate was their goal.

THE FINAL GOAL.

On arriving at the bottom of the hill, the open space was comparatively free. The shops in the locality were almost without exception closed. Many of them had not that morning been opened ; and where the shutters had been taken down, they were hastily replaced. Behind half-opened doors the proprietors stood bending their heads forward to catch a glimpse of the terrible intruders ; and at the corners of every street were small groups of persons scarcely daring to show themselves, each trying to conceal himself behind others of the group, and all ready in a moment to dart from sight into a place of safety. Few ventured to expose themselves on the pavement. Sweeping round in a semi-circle to the right from the foot of the hill, the head of the Chartist body moved forward until it reached the gates at the entrance to the stable-yard of the Hotel, some of the party as they swept round pointing their guns threateningly at the windows. The gates had been securely fastened, and therefore ingress was found impracticable. Being thus frustrated in what apparently they had contemplated, Frost, addressing them, said, "Show your appearance in the front," upon which some of the leaders went to the front door of the hostelry, inside which were stationed Mr. Hopkins (the Superintendent of Police), Mr. T. B. Oliver (a printer), Mr. Henry Williams, Mr. Benjamin Gould, Mr. O'Dwyer, Mr. Venn, and a number of the most valiant of the special constables. The Mayor had countermanded his first order as to closing the door, and had subsequently directed that the door should remain open, but that certain constables should be placed in charge, and allow no one to enter. The movements of the Chartists were for a few moments witnessed by the Mayor from an upstairs room ; but, deeming his presence necessary below, he ran down, and on reaching the bar saw the head of the column by the doorway. He passed on to communicate with Lieutenant Grey.

THE ATTACK.

On approaching the front door, the leaders of the Chartists were asked what they wanted, upon which they grounded their arms and made some demand relative to the surrender of prisoners. By some it is alleged that the words "Surrender yourselves as prisoners" were used; but others maintain that the expression was "Surrender our prisoners," alluding to the men who, during the night, had been taken into custody. Whatever the purport of the expression, however, a reply was made by Mr. Henry Williams, "What prisoners?" A constable, more bold than his fellows, replied, with Stentorian voice, "No, never!" At the same time an attempt was made to seize a pike in the hands of one of the Chartists, upon which a gun was immediately levelled and fired at the head of the first constable, a man named Thomas Bevan Oliver, a printer of the town. Seeing the danger, he immediately slammed the door, and succeeded in striking aside the barrel of the gun as it exploded, so that the shot took no effect. The constables made no attack, as they had been particularly ordered by the Mayor to act only on the defensive.

The firing of the first gun seemed to have dissipated the courage of the special constables, who were armed only with staves, and to have incited the Chartists to a general and indiscriminate attack upon the Hotel. "In, my men!" was the command uttered by one John Lovell and others, and a rush into the building was the work of a moment. The passage was speedily choked, and then many made ingress through the windows. The constables fled in all directions—some to the cellars, some to upstair rooms, others to the yard and outhouses, while the more nimble mounted the walls and roofs, and made their way to their homes or other places of security, where they changed their clothes, fearing that being police officers they would be shot. It is jocularly said that, some time after the conclusion of the affray, one of the brave defenders was discovered, with his baton of authority, snugly ensconced in the copper boiler. More than one constable, however, was severely wounded, and, being unable to escape, was left to the tender mercy of the rebels. Henry Williams (ironmonger), whose name we have before mentioned, was wounded at the commencement of the attack. He received a gunshot wound in the head, a wound in the leg, and two stabs in the body. He fell senseless, and was left alone. It was fortunate he escaped with his life. Mr. Hallen, the landlord of the Hotel, whilst escorting some ladies upstairs, was struck and wounded by a slug. A constable named Morgan (draper, of Waterloo House, Commercial Street), was also wounded by a gunshot, afterwards abstracted. Among a number of special constables stationed in the commercial room of the Hotel were Mr. Thomas Latch, Mr. Waters (an attorney), and a Mr. Cleave, whose anxious curiosity induced them to peep through the crevices of the shutters of the window overlooking the bottom of Stow

Hill. Immediately on being noticed, the passing Chartists dashed their weapons through the glass, the hinder ones completing the destruction which the foremost ranks had commenced. The valour of the constables was shown in its better part discretion; and when danger was apprehended from this proceeding, they fled from the room with the intention of escaping by the back way. Mr. Latch succeeded, but Mr. Waters, after a moment's delay, found to his dismay that the head of the column had intruded itself into the house, and that the doorways and passages were all blockaded. Waters, as a *dernier ressort*, dashed upstairs, and, succeeding in gaining access to a back room of the building, remained there until all danger passed away. The men who thus filled the passages of the house, ere the smoke of the first guns cleared away, appeared bent on destroying all property, thrusting their pikes at the glass, and attempting to smash everything within reach. Outside, the windows were broken, and frequent shots fired into the various rooms of the building. The shutters of the room in which the soldiers were stationed were battered by weapons which, from the inside, could be seen above the closed shutters, and torn by slugs and balls fired at them.

THE DEFENCE.

The Mayor and Lieutenant Grey found it was time to act, and accordingly the soldiers were ordered to load with ball cartridge. As they were in the act of loading, shots were heard in the passage which communicated with the room and other parts of the house, and in a very short time the soldiers would have found themselves between two fires. The door was temporarily secured, and the Mayor and Lieutenant Grey went to open the windows to enable the soldiers to fire therefrom. Lieutenant Grey stood at the middle window of the bay, and the Mayor at the window nearest the centre of the building. At the same moment they withdrew, and the soldiers approached and fired upon the mob. Before they could do so, however, the Mayor found that he had been wounded in his arm by a slug; and from the holes in his trousers, he knew that he had also received a shot in his groin or hip. The wound in the arm proved to be a very severe one; the wound in the hip was only a flesh wound. Sergeant Daily was also wounded by six slugs in the head, and had also the pan of his gun knocked away by a ball from the Chartists as he was in the act of loading. The firing of the soldiers soon proved effective, and the shrieks of the dying and wounded men among the mob created a panic. In a few moments it was evident the mob was scampering away in all directions. A few reckless spirits among them, however, continued to return the fire of the soldiers, and seemed to court death at their hands in the most daring manner. One man named George Turner, conspicuous by the fact of his having a wooden leg, continued to load and fire time after time; and whether the soldiers out of pity for his deformity, or whether from mere accident, the fact remains that he stood almost alone as a target for their fire, and yet escaped uninjured.

After firing the first few volleys, the soldiers had to turn for their own protection to repel the attack made in the passage to obtain an entrance into the room. A caution having been given to any special constables who might have been in the way, the door was opened, and the fire of the soldiers now poured into the passage. In such close quarters the shots could hardly fail to prove fatal, and here the dead and wounded fell thick together. The intruders, probably unconscious of what had occurred in the street, and that their commander had fled, again and again made a dash to get into the room; but each time they advanced they were met by the steady and deadly fire of the soldiers, which added to the number of killed and wounded, until the streams of blood flowing at their feet, the piercing shrieks of their comrades, and the obstacle to progress formed by the helpless bodies, made them recoil in horror.

During the affray the Mayor had another very narrow escape of his life. Finding the blood from his arm flowing so fast as to induce him to think there was danger from the hemorrhage, he went to a special constable, who he saw in the passage, and asked him to bind up his arm. While he was endeavouring to do this, one of the insurgents made his appearance, and prepared to thrust his pike at them; but, before he could do this, he was shot by one of the soldiers, and fell on his face at their feet, apparently dying. Again, when the Mayor was returning to his room, after the blood from the wound in his arm was staunched, a soldier approached the door, and, not being able to distinguish him through the smoke, presented his musket within a few feet of his head. Lobbett, the constable, who had bound up the Mayor's arm, seeing this, called out "For God's sake, don't fire; it is the Mayor!" The soldier immediately threw up his musket, and the Mayor entered the room.

THE COLLAPSE.

In about ten minutes danger was over, and Lieutenant Grey ordered his men to cease firing. At length the spot was deserted, the dead and dying only being left where, but a few minutes before, such terrible commotion had existed. The Mayor and the soldiers then left the room; the former being compelled, by the state of his wounds, to relinquish his authority and the preservation of the peace of the town into other hands.

Mr. Blewitt, who, after addressing the Chartists at Llantarnam, rode into Newport through Caerleon, consented, at the Mayor's request, to remain in the town and take his place. [Pencilled in the margin of the MS. of the Mayor's statement are these words: "Contemptible trickery to deprive a brave man of his meed of praise."] Sergeant Daily remained in bed at the Westgate for a day, and was then removed to the residence of the Mayor, where, with his wife, he remained for thirteen days, receiving during that time every attention from the Mayor, his sister, and family. [In the margin of Daily's statement, taken on the 30th November, 1839, is this annotation of probably a facetious counsel: "Hem! Thirteen days' board and lodging for one knight!"—an allusion to the honour subsequently conferred upon the Mayor.]

The soldiers, on the average, fired three rounds each; but many of them entirely exhausted their stock of ammunition, and a further supply was deemed absolutely necessary. There was a difficulty how to obtain more. No soldier could leave his post, and no other person in the house was willing to stir. Yes! there was one person—a young volunteer, a small boy named Partridge (our esteemed townsman, Mr. W. H. F. Partridge), who expressed his willingness to run to the Barracks and bring the ammunition. He was permitted to go, and in a very short time returned with his pockets loaded with cartridges. It was a valourous act, but for which the lad was never rewarded.

The collapse of this great movement, which had filled the hearts of thousands with terror, was as sudden as unexpected. Literally an army fled before a mere handful of disciplined soldiers, whom they could not even see. The flight of the rebels was swift, and prolonged until safety was obtained in seclusion. Many of the men threw away their arms, and even their outer garments, in order to assist them in making their escape the quicker.

From the time that the leading force passed down Stow Hill until they retraced their steps over the same ground but a few minutes had transpired. In fact the rear, accompanied by Zephaniah Williams, had scarcely commenced the descent of the hill ere they were met by those whom conscience or terror had put to flight.

THE FLIGHT.

Zephaniah Williams soon perceived the hasty retreat, and heard of the disaster to his cause. It was a sudden shock to all his hopes; he made no attempt by hurrying on his forces to retrieve the position, the unwilling ones were troubled no more, and every one joined in the general flight. Williams gave way to despair, and was one of the first to seek his own personal safety. In a very short time the driver of the tram, who had brought him from Llanhilleth, met him at Waterloo.

The head of the retreating party soon reached the Park, but the intelligence which the first few brought was scarcely believed. Upon the report reaching the ears of the poor fellow Lloyd, who was pushed into the canal at Abercarn, he again made an attempt to regain his liberty; but his guardian, with a curse, once more threatened him. Every instant, however, the persons hastening from Newport increased in numbers. They all brought the same disastrous information, the dire results becoming even much exaggerated as the tale was conveyed from man to man.

CHARTIST RIOTS.

It was not long before Frost himself was recognised hastening at a good strong pace along the road, holding with his left hand a handkerchief to his face, and apparently crying. Being recognised by one of the park-keepers, named William Adams, he was asked what was the matter; but he stopped not, and the reply he made was unintelligible. The curiosity of the park-keeper was aroused. He was not altogether ignorant of the entry of the Chartists into Newport; but, seeing them now flying back in droves, and Frost among their number, he conjectured that the fortunes of the day were against them. Turning upon his horse, he followed Frost, and saw him enter a piece of copse wood running under the park wall at a distance of about three hundred yards from the lodge gate.

Beyond the park and upward in the tramroad from Pye Corner, the retreat continued; and guns, pikes, and mandrils, thrown away, marked the course taken by the rebels.

On the road to the Cefn, the same scene was presented, and again repeated on the fields and paths leading to the heights of Penylan Vawr. Here William Jones, at ten o'clock, was idly waiting, when man after man came rushing, despondent and fatigued, yet eagerly hastening onward. Jones enquired what had occurred in Newport, and was informed that an attack had been made on the Westgate Hotel, that three or four men had been killed, and that the whole body were defeated. Jones exclaimed, "Oh! damn me; then we are done!" Beyond the crowd gathered around him, the news soon spread, but the outburst of grief or passion was not of long duration. The rabble became, if possible, more disorderly than ever. Jones lost all control over them, and in a very short time the spot was deserted, every man making the best of his way to his own home.

There was no pursuit of the rebels, nor any attempt to make prisoners of any numbers; nor was there any pursuit necessary to hasten their flight. Oaths and curses resounded on all sides, and the bitterness of feeling was now turned by the deluded men upon those who had acted as their leaders. Along every road, every field, and under every hedge were now seen the units of this immense force dispersed like chaff before the wind.

AFTER THE CONFLICT.

In front of the Westgate alone about 150 weapons of various kinds, thrown down by the Chartists, were collected together, and subsequently removed to Cross House, on Stow Hill, the residence of Mr. Hopkins, the Superintendent of the Borough Police Force. Among these being guns, pistols, blunderbusses, swords, bayonets, daggers, pikes, spears, billhooks, reaping hooks, hatchets, cleavers, axes, pitchforks, blades of knives, scythes and saws fixed in staves; rods of iron, two and three yards in length, sharpened at one end; bludgeons of various length and size, hand and sledge hammers, and mandrils; in fact every implement that could be made available as a weapon.

Inside the Westgate five dead bodies were found weltering in their blood. Two unwounded Chartists found in the house were secured as prisoners. Every attention was speedily given to the wounded in the house. Medical men were sent for, and all those at hand gave their services readily. Mr. R. F. Woollett and Mr. Jehoiada Brewer were among the number who were present on the occasion. As the doors remained fastened, access to the building was only obtained through the windows; and we have heard on good authority that as the former gentleman was being assisted headforemost through the opened window space, the one predominant thought in his mind was what an excellent target he presented for any Chartist who might still be lingering in the vicinity.

The wounded men—and there were many of them—managed to escape. One man named Lovell, who carried a gun and was wounded in the thigh, lay near the corner of Skinner Street for some time, repeatedly calling for assistance. At length several persons carried him away to the house of a Mr. Jenkins, where he was put to bed and his wound attended to.

One dead man was lying under the portico of the Mayor's house at the foot of Stow Hill. He received a gunshot wound when at the corner of the Westgate, and, falling upon his hands and knees, crept across the road, and fell where his body was found. Mr. Benjamin Evans, of the London House, and the late Father Metcalf endeavoured to render him some assistance, but they were driven off by the threats of the soldiers, and the misguided man died where he fell, exclaiming, "The Charter for ever!" Another body was lying on the steps near the doorway of the Westgate, apparently shot at the moment of entering the Hotel.

The dead bodies were not permitted to be removed during the whole day. Many persons—some from mere curiosity, and others from nobler motives—attempted to go towards them; but as soon as they ventured to approach, the guns of the soldiers still on guard were levelled at them, and the attempt was in no case persisted in. Eventually the dead bodies were removed on stretchers, and laid out in the stables of the Hotel to await an inquest. On their being examined it was found that nearly all were well supplied with ammunition, loose slugs, ball cartridges, and powder in flasks. Among the dead the following were identified:—William Williams, of Cwmtillery; George Shell, of Pontypool; Abraham Thomas, of Coalbrook Vale; William Evans, of Tredegar; Isaac Thomas, of Nantyglo; William Griffiths, of Merthyr; William Farraday, of Blackwood.

Shell was only 19 years of age, and by trade a cabinetmaker. That he was an enthusiast in what he believed to be a good cause,

CHARTIST RIOTS.

is proved by the following letter, which was found in his box after his death :—

"Pontypool, Sunday Night, November 4th, 1839.

"Dear Parents,—I hope this will find you well, as I am myself at present. I shall this night be engaged in a struggle for freedom, and should it please God to spare my life, I shall see you soon; but if not, grieve not for me. I shall fall in a noble cause. My tools are at Mr. Cecil's, and likewise my clothes.

"Yours truly,

"GEORGE SHELL."

It is said that Shell was the man shot down in the passage by one of the soldiers when he attempted to take the life of the Mayor.

The dead body of one David Morgan was said to have been laid out on a table in a house down towards Friars Fields.

Altogether 22 bodies were discovered, but not one identified as belonging to Newport.

As may be expected, many scenes of withering woe were observed, and the record of one may be regarded as an instance of others. A young woman, who had forced her way through the crowd of spectators in the stable-yard, no sooner came within sight of the dead than she threw herself upon one of the bodies—her husband! She was tenderly dragged from him, smeared with his blood upon her face and arms.

The bodies of the Chartists were subsequently interred in St. Woolos Churchyard, on the north side of St. Mary's Chapel.

So great a consternation did the event occasion in the town, that it is recorded a woman was prematurely taken in labour, and died in child-birth.

PERSONAL EXPERIENCES.

The father of the Mayor—an infirm old gentleman—endeavoured to seek safety by mounting a ladder and scaling a wall; but so helpless was the old gentleman that he was found on the wall unable to advance or retire. He was removed with the greatest difficulty by the assistance of his servant and others who found him in this position.

Many interesting incidents are still remembered by several inhabitants of the town now living. Mr. Henry Mullock, printer, witnessed the attack upon the Hotel from an upstairs window of the premises of Mr. Webber (now Mr. Alfred Taylor, outfitter), when a shot struck the window blind near. Himself and companions at once bolted down Skinner Street and up Corn Street, towards his house; but in that brief space of time the rioters had gone! He ventured to visit several poor fellows lying on the pavement, but was at once ordered off by the soldiers then stationed in the offices of Messrs. Prothero and Phillips, at the bottom of Stow Hill.

Mr. Mullock's father, when the attack was made, was standing at his shop door (the premises being the same as now occupied by his son) talking to Mr. Davies, proprietor of the London House. This establishment had been promptly closed by the assistants (of whom Mr. Benjamin Evans was one) on learning of the advance of the Chartists down the hill; but Mr. Mullock's shop remained open, as did that of his neighbour, Mr. William Evans. While Mr. Mullock and Mr. Davies were engaged in earnest conversation a bullet whizzed near their heads, and lodged in the wall adjoining Mr. Evans's shop.

Mr. W. H. F. Partridge, shortly before the riots, assisted his father in a furniture warehouse, kept by him at that time. A customer one day entered and purchased two dozen chairs, to be sent by the tram to Blaina. In looking round the warehouse he espied some sword belts and pistols (which had just been received for the use of the West Monmouthshire Yeomanry), and enquired if they were for sale. On being informed that they were not to be disposed of, he asked what they were for, when the lad bluntly told him he thought they were "to tackle the Chartists with." When the lad's father returned home, he heard of what had transpired, and discovered that his customer for chairs was no other than Zephaniah Williams, of Blaina—one of the Chartist leaders!

About nine o'clock on Monday morning a rumour was set afloat in Pontypool that the Chartists had secured possession of Newport, and that the soldiers were all killed. Upon this many of the Chartist women set off towards the town in the hope of gaining plunder; and it is recorded that they appeared more eager than the men. The real state of affairs was not known in the town until two o'clock in the afternoon.

APPREHENSION OF THE LEADERS.

As soon as the authorities saw that danger in Newport had ceased, they lost no time in taking the necessary legal steps to bring to justice the leaders of this great public outrage. Before the day closed warrants were issued for their apprehension, and also warrants for the search of their dwellings, and the dwellings of others who were known or suspected to be concerned in the affair. Placards, offering a reward of £100 for the apprehension of either of the leaders named, were also issued. At five o'clock in the evening, the Superintendent of Police, with Mr. Thomas Jones Phillips (solicitor), and a Mr. Stephen Rogers, went to Frost's house. The servant opened the door, and they were shown into a room behind the shop, where Mrs. Frost immediately attended them. Having ascertained that Mr. Frost was not at home, they explained to Mrs. Frost their business, and commenced minutely to examine all the papers they could procure. In this examination they were readily assisted by Mrs. Frost and several of the daughters, who attended the officers the whole of the time they were in the house. The papers were in no way concealed, but openly placed upon shelves in a room in which it was the practice of Mr. Frost to receive persons who applied to him on magisterial business. The papers were taken from the shelves, bundle after bundle, by Miss Frost, and handed to the officers for inspection.

From Frost's they proceeded to the house of a printer, named Partridge, who lived near what is now known as Devon Place. Partridge, it was known had been much employed by Frost in printing his productions, and it was expected that some criminatory matters would be obtained from him.

A knock at the door was made, but no notice was taken of the knocking by any one inside. An attempt being then made to open the door from the outside, it was found to be fastened. Mr. Partridge was called upon by name, upon which a voice inside said, "I am gone to bed." He was directed at once to get up, and come down and open the door, and informed that unless he did so the door would be forced open. There was no response made to the appeal, and therefore steps were at once taken to force an entrance. In a very few minutes the iron fastenings on the inside were heard to fall, and the door was opened. As soon as this was effected, the sergeant of police, much to his astonishment, saw Mr. Frost in the house standing within two yards of the doorway. A well-known Chartist named Charles Waters (ship's carpenter) was also there. Partridge was in the same room with them. Mr. Phillips and Mr. Rogers at once seized Frost, and told him he must consider himself a prisoner. Frost merely replied, "Very well; I will go with you directly." They were, however, not prepared instantly to take him, and said he must wait a little. The officers thereupon proceeded in execution of the warrant to search Partridge's premises. Partridge handed to Mr. Phillips two files of manuscript; and while the latter was examining them, Frost walked across and asked by what authority he examined the papers. Mr. Phillips told him that he did not think it necessary to make him acquainted with his authority, upon which Mr. Frost added, "If you expect to find any of my MS. there, you are mistaken." Frost appeared much fatigued and depressed, and complained of being very uncomfortable; so as soon as the search was completed, he took Mr. Phillips's arm, and they walked together to the Westgate. Waters followed in custody also, although there was no warrant at that moment against him. While at the Westgate both prisoners were searched; and on the former were found three new pistols, a flask nearly full of powder, and some balls. One of the pistols was of larger size than the other two. All three were loaded, but the caps had been taken off. [Two of these pistols are now in the Museum of the Newport Free Library, having been presented by Mr. Jones Phillips, son of the gentleman who took them from Mr. Frost's possession.] Upon Waters were found four pistols, a powder flask, and between 40 and 50 balls, together with matches, loose in his pocket. All the pistols were loaded with ball.

CHARTIST RIOTS.

Frost and Waters were kept under a guard of soldiers that night at the Westgate, and next day were brought before the local magistrates. Mr. William Truman Harford Phelps, solicitor, of Newport, appeared for the prosecution. At the conclusion of the investigation, they were committed for trial at the Assizes on a charge of high treason. On the following day (Wednesday) they were removed to Monmouth, under an escort of the 10th Hussars as far as Usk, when a party of the 12th Lancers took charge of them, and conveyed them to Monmouth. Jones was apprehended at Crumlin, about a week after the attack. Zephaniah Williams eluded capture for ten days. In the meantime he had shipped at Cardiff on board the barque *Vintage*, bound for Oporto, in the name of Thomas Jones. He was discovered sleeping in his berth, and taken into custody.

Beside the leaders here named, ten others—namely, James Aust, Edmund Edmunds, Richard Benfield, John Rees, John Lovell, John Rees (*alias* Jack the Fifer), Solomon Brittan, Jenkin Morgan, George Turner, and David Jones (*alias* David the Tinker)—were committed, and subsequently indicted for high treason; and about thirty others, for minor offences, including John Partridge, George George, Samuel Etheridge, Benjamin Richards, Evan Edwards, Thomas Llewellin, John Owen, and John Gibby.

The magisterial investigations continued at the Westgate for 24 days, and no less than 160 witnesses were examined. The Rev. James Coles presided; and the other magistrates constantly in attendance were Octavius Morgan, Esq., Mr. W. S. Cartwright, Mr. R. J. Blewitt, Mr. G. Hall, Mr. W. Brewer, and Mr. Thomas Hawkins. Mr. Octavius Morgan was on the Continent when the news reached him of the disturbances, and he at once made a rapid journey home.

Israel Firman, a witness admitted to give evidence at Newport on the part of the Crown, was a notability who occasioned much attention. His attenuated and sapless form produced a mingled sensation of wonder and dread in the Court. His unearthly aspect had so excited the fears of the ignorant in the neighbourhood that he was popularly regarded as a Sorcerer. Tall, gaunt, and withered, he stood upright, though exceeding 90 years of age. A profusion of long grisly hair, flung back from his wrinkled and projecting forehead, gave an expression of great wildness to his features; while his sunken and hollow cheeks, shelving eyebrows, piercing and jet-black eyes, conspired to render his apparition in Court a thing not to be forgotten. His deeply sunburnt complexion and indistinct Asiatic pronunciation strongly favoured the opinion that he belonged to the outcast and wandering progeny of Ishmael.

He was generally known as a quack doctor, conjuror, and fortune-teller; but in his evidence on oath, he stated:—" I shall be 91 years of age in May next. Was apprenticed to a herbalist in Philadelphia. Was pressed in Antigua, 1789, by Lieutenant Byng, of the Berbice tender. Came to England 1816. Since being discharged, gained living by grinding scissors."

ISRAEL FIRMAN.

In the meantime Newport was made the headquarters of a large military force, and had all the appearance of a garrison town. Six hundred troops, including artillery, were quartered here and in the district; companies of troops being sent to the chief towns and places where the disaffected had appeared in numbers.

The magistrates at Pontypool held sittings, and sent for trial large numbers of persons for riot and illegal assembly; and also William Shellard, for high treason.

At Cardiff the Mayor, magistrates, and naval and military officers of the neighbourhood, assembled the pensioners; got four field pieces and a few cannonades into position, to protect the town.

On the 9th of November, Lord Normanbury conveyed to Mr. Phillips, the Mayor, a written expression of the Queen's approval of the conduct of the Mayor and magistrates; on the 13th followed this up with an offer of Knighthood for the Mayor—Sir Thomas Phillips—who was afterwards Knighted at Windsor Castle.

Several persons who had been wounded—namely, Walker, Williams, Morgan, &c.—were rewarded with pensions for life. These are now all deceased.

TRIALS OF THE PRISONERS.

On the 19th of November a Special Commission of Oyer and Terminer, issued under the Great Seal of the United Kingdom, was held; and a Special Commission of Gaol Delivery, as to all persons who were or should be in custody for such offences, on or before the 11th day of December following.

On the 10th December the Special Commissions were opened in the Crown Court at Monmouth at ten o'clock, the judges being the Right Hon. the Lord Chief Justice Tindal; the Right Hon. Mr. Baron Parkes, and the Hon. Mr. Justice Williams. The Lord Lieutenant of the County, Capel Hanbury Leigh, Esq., was also present.

The Court-house inside was crowded, while outside the town was in a state of great excitement. Every precaution had been taken by the authorities for the safe custody of the prisoners; and to prevent the possibility of any disturbance, the constabulary force was largely augmented and detachments of military were located in the town. In apprehension of possible contingencies, alterations were made in the ancient structure which stands upon the bridge at Over Monnow, and loop holes were pierced in such positions as to enable troops stationed within to fire upon any person approaching.

Immediately after the Commissions were read, the Court adjourned until one o'clock, when the sheriff, Colthurst Bateman, Esq., of Pertholey, delivered in the jury panel comprising about 260 names.

The following gentlemen were ultimately sworn as the Grand Jury:—

Lord Granville Charles Henry Somerset, foreman,
The Hon. William Rodney,
Sir Benjamin Hall, Bart.
Wm. Addams Williams, Esq.,
Reginald James Blewitt, Esq.,
Richard Amphlett, Esq.,
Joseph Bailey, Esq.,
Richard Blakemore, Esq.,
Francis Chambre, Esq.,
William Curre, Esq.,
Philip John Ducarel, Esq.,
Joseph Davies, Esq.,
John Gisborne, Esq.,
Samuel Homfray, Esq.,
John Francis Vaughan, Esq.,
John Jenkins, Esq.,
Thomas Lewis, Esq.,
Charles Octavius Swinnerton Morgan, Esq.,
Charles Marriott, Esq.,
Francis McDonnell, Esq.,
Joseph Needham, Esq.,
Charles Harrison Powell, Esq.,
John Ethrington Welsh Rolls, Esq.

The Lord Chief Justice, in charging the Grand Jury, expounded the law which defined and applied to charges of high treason, and explained the proof necessary to constitute the offence. High

treason, said the learned Chief Justice, in its own direct consequences, is calculated to produce the most malignant effects upon the community at large; its direct and immediate tendency is the putting down the authority of the land, the shaking and subverting the foundation of all government, the loosening and dissolving the bonds and cement by which society is held together, the general confusion of property, and the involving a whole people in bloodshed and mutual destruction. Accordingly, high treason had always been regarded by the law of this country as the offence of all others of the deepest dye, and as calling for the severest measure of punishment.

Not until the following day, at three o'clock, did the Grand Jury return a true bill of High Treason against John Frost, Charles Waters, Richard Benfield, George Turner (otherwise called George Cole), John Rees, James Aust, Zephaniah Williams, Jenkin Morgan, William Jones, John Lovell, Edmund Edmunds, Solomon Brittan, one other John Rees, and David Jones.

The prisoners were then placed at the bar, and informed that a true bill of High Treason had been found against them by the Grand Jury.

Upon the application of the prisoners, the Court directed that copies of the indictment should be furnished to them; and on the motion of Mr. Wightman, the Court ordered that the Sheriff should deliver to Mr. Maule, solicitor for the Treasury, a copy of the jury panel.

It is important to record here, as having an important bearing upon a subsequent part of the case, that on the 12th December a copy of the indictment and a list of the jurors was delivered to each of the prisoners by Mr. Maule; and on the 17th December a list of witnesses was delivered to them.

The trials commenced on Tuesday, the 31st December, before the learned Judges already named. The counsel for the Crown were the Attorney-General (Sir John Campbell), the Solicitor-General (Sir Thomas Wilde), Mr. Sergeant Ludlow, Mr. Sergeant Talfourd and Mr. Wightman (both subsequently raised to the Bench), and the Hon. J. C. Talbot.

At the request of Mr. Frost, Sir Frederick Pollock and Mr. Fitzroy Kelly were assigned as his counsel; Mr. Thomas being assistant counsel; and Mr. W. F. Geach, solicitor.

The indictment against the prisoners comprised four counts, the substance of their charge being that they had broken their faith and true allegiance to the Sovereign, and levied war against her within her realm. The first two counts of the indictment were founded upon the ancient statute of 25 Edward III., the remaining two counts being founded upon the modern Act 36 George III., c. 7.

On the prisoners being arraigned, they severally pleaded "Not guilty."

CHARTIST RIOTS.

The council for John Frost having stated that they intended on his behalf to sever in the challenges, and the other prisoners having in answer to a question from the Court severally expressed the same intention, the Attorney-General stated that he should proceed first with the trial of John Frost.

In consideration of his having been recently unwell, he was allowed the indulgence of a seat.

The Clerk of Assize then proceeded to call those jurors who had answered to their names upon the first calling over of the panel :—

John Daniel, Abergavenny, haberdasher, sworn (foreman).
Thomas Davies, Abergavenny, butcher, sworn.
Richard Lewis, Llanvair Discoed, farmer, sworn.
Edward Brittle, Mitcheltroy, farmer, sworn.
James Hollings, Monmouth, ironmonger, sworn.
Thomas Jones, Great House, Nash, farmer, sworn.
Edward Reece, Llanmartin, miller, sworn.
Edward Smith, Chepstow, coachmaker, sworn.
Christopher John, Redwick, farmer, sworn.
William Williams, Llangattock-nigh-Usk, farmer, sworn.
John Richards, Chepstow, baker, sworn.
John Capel Smith, Chepstow, grocer, sworn.
Daniel Walters, of Redwick, farmer, was challenged by prisoner.
John Jones, Itton, farmer, challenged by prisoner.
William Crump, Abergavenny, victualler, challenged by prisoner.
William James, Itton, farmer, challenged by prisoner.
Henry Jones, Chepstow, butcher, was proved to be not qualified.
Walter Davies, Llangattock-nigh-Usk, farmer, challenged by prisoner.
John Collins, Christchurch, farmer, challenged by prisoner.
Matthew Cope, Caerleon, maltster, challenged by prisoner.
Edward Jones, Caerleon, flour factor, challenged by prisoner.
Charles Williams, Redwick, farmer, challenged by prisoner.
Walter Lewis Mathern, farmer, challenged by prisoner.
James Long, Llanvaches, farmer, challenged by prisoner.
Rees Davies, Chepstow, draper, challenged by prisoner.
Thomas Davis, Chepstow, gentleman, challenged by prisoner.
Edward Davis, Tintern Parva, farmer, challenged by the Attorney-General on the part of the Crown.
John Linus, Abergavenny, grocer, challenged by prisoner.
Thomas Swift, Monmouth, timber merchant, challenged by prisoner.
Thomas Iles, Tintern Parva, farmer, challenged by prisoner.
Charles Hall, Nash, farmer, challenged by prisoner.
William Jones, Nash, farmer, challenged by prisoner.
James O'Hare, Monmouth, grocer, challenged by prisoner.
John Roberts, Shirenewton, miller, challenged by prisoner.
Richard Reece, Rockfield, farmer, challenged by prisoner.
James Rosser, Penhow, farmer, challenged by prisoner.
John Reece, Llanmartin, miller, challenged by prisoner.

CHARTIST RIOTS. 53

Isaac Hurcum, Chepstow, butcher, challenged by prisoner.
James Powles, Raglan, farmer, challenged by prisoner.
Thomas John, Nash, farmer, challenged by prisoner.
Edward Williams, Llandavenny, farmer, challenged by prisoner.
Cradock Gwynne Watkins, of Llangwm-ucha, farmer, challenged by prisoner.
William James, Goldcliff, farmer, challenged by prisoner.
John Bowcott, Abergavenny, victualler, challenged by Crown.
Samuel Churchill, Llanllowell, gentleman, challenged by prisoner.
Philip Bennet, Penhow, farmer, challenged by prisoner.
James Young, Christchurch, innkeeper and farmer, challenged by prisoner.
William Henry James, Caerleon, tanner, challenged by prisoner.
George Baker, Abergavenny, cooper, challenged by prisoner.
Joseph Waters, Nash, farmer, challenged by prisoner.
William Seys, Llanvaplcy, farmer, challenged by prisoner.
George Adams, Portskewett, tailor, challenged by Crown.
Charles Boucher Howells, Abergavenny, cornfactor, challenged by prisoner.
David Davies, Raglan, farmer, challenged by Crown.
Isaac Williams, Usk, saddler, challenged by Crown.
William Jones, Abergavenny, tailor, challenged by Crown.
Charles Charles, Tintern Parva, innkeeper, challenged by Crown.

About thirty were fined £10 each for not answering.

The first twelve gentlemen above named having at length been sworn as the jury, they were charged with the prisoner, in the usual form, and the court adjourned until the following morning, Wednesday, January 1st, 1840.

On the assembly of the Court, Sir Frederick Pollock availed himself of the earliest opportunity to make an objection which, he stated, must be made sooner or later, and before a single witness was put into the box. As the Attorney-General was about making a statement that must be painful to himself, painful to all in Court, and perhaps prejudicial to the Crown and to the prisoner, he thought it the proper thing to make the objection and not to permit such a statement to be made. The objection was that the prisoner had not had a list of witnesses delivered to him pursuant to the statute.

The Attorney-General, on being appealed to by the Court, said he was prepared to prove the contrary; upon which

The Lord Chief Justice said the Court could not then interpose, and the Attorney-General proceeded to state his case to the jury. He briefly stated that there had recently been in the county an armed insurrection; the law had been set at defiance; an attempt had been made to take forcible possession of the town of Newport; there had been a conflict between the insurgents and the Queen's troops, and there had been bloodshed and the loss of many lives. Not only from the importance of these events, which had caused alarm and dismay throughout the kingdom, but from the forms of law required in connection with such charges, there was a necessity to have a Special Commission. He then explained that the indictment contained four counts : the first two being for levying war against her Majesty in her realm ; the third for compassing to depose the Queen ; and the fourth for compassing to levy war against the Queen with intent to compel her to change her measures. The Act of Edward III., which defined treasonable offences, was then explained, and then the particular circumstances in which the prisoner had been engaged were briefly narrated.

At the conclusion of the address,

Samuel Simmons was called, when

Sir F. Pollock renewed his objection that no list of witnesses had been delivered in pursuance of the Act of Parliament.

The Attorney-General, to prove that this had been done, called George Maule, Esq., the solicitor for the affairs of H.M. Treasury, who had the conduct of the prosecution. On being sworn, he deposed that he delivered to the prisoner Frost a copy of the indictment, with a list of the jury, on the 12th December, in the afternoon, and that on the 17th December he had delivered a list of the witnesses.

Sir F. Pollock now stated the nature of his objection, which was that the list of witnesses should not only have been delivered ten days before the trial, but also at the same time with a copy of the indictment and the list of the jury, in accordance with the Act 7th Anne, cap. 21, sec. 11.

The Attorney-General contended that the meaning of the Act had been most fully and amply complied with, and that the prisoner had had all the advantage which the Legislature intended he should enjoy. And further, that the objection should have been made at the time of prisoner's arraignment, when, if allowed, the whole effect would have been to postpone the trial for ten days.

Before concluding his argument, the Attorney-General was stopped, and the learned Judges having consulted together for a few minutes,

Lord Chief Justice Tindal said they were not prepared to say that the objection made by prisoner's counsel was valid ; but it involved a question upon which no direct decision had taken place, and which called for very serious consideration. They proposed to take a course which would prevent the possibility of an overhasty decision operating to the disadvantage of the prisoner, and, on the other hand, from causing a failure of public justice. They would allow the trial to proceed, and they would take the opinion of Her Majesty's Judges on the validity of the objection, supposing such proceeding should become necessary by the verdict of the jury.

The Court then adjourned, with an intimation that they would on the following morning proceed with the evidence.

CHARTIST RIOTS.

On the assembling of the Court on Thursday, 2nd January, 1840, Sir Frederick Pollock endeavoured to elicit from the Court as to the position of the prisoner if the objection which he had made should by the Court at Westminster be held to be valid.

Some testy remarks passed between the opposing counsel, but the Lord Chief Justice very cautiously decided that if the Court were of opinion that the objection ought to have prevailed, the position of Mr. Frost would be as if it had prevailed at the moment.

Samuel Simmons was then sworn, when the minor objection as to the witness's description was made by Sir Frederick Pollock. The witness was described as of the parish of St. Woolos, in the borough of Newport. In cross-examination, the witness made the following statements, which we extract, as throwing some light upon the then condition of the town:—I live just below the Inn or Public-house called the Salutation. The Salutation stands on a piece of waste ground at the side of Cardiff Street; at the side of the street that goes down to Pill. My house is a little below the Salutation; you turn on the right; it is on the tramroad that the coals and iron go down by. There is no other road than the tramroad. There are about a dozen houses in the same place. There is a place below that used to be called Mountjoy; I do not know any name to the street. The house is about a quarter of a mile from the Westgate Inn. There are houses all the way from the Westgate Inn to the Salutation. There are houses all the way from the Salutation to the house where I live. I never heard any name to the place. It never had any name to it. I never in my life had any letters directed to me; nor anybody near me that I know of. My house is neither rated to the poor rate nor to the borough rate. It is only £6 a year. The tramway goes all the way up to the Hills.

The prisoner's counsel very ably argued that the description furnished of the witness was a misdescription, and insufficient, inasmuch as he was described of the parish of St. Woolos in the borough of Newport, whereas, in fact, the parish of St. Woolos was not within the borough of Newport, but, on the contrary, the borough of Newport was within the parish of St. Woolos, and formed part of it.

The Boundary Act was referred to, and witnesses called to prove the fact.

Ultimately the Court overruled the objection, the Lord Chief Justice holding that the description given of the witness was true in every fact and particular. The other Judges severally delivered their opinion to the same effect.

The following witnesses were then examined:—

Thomas Morris, land surveyor, proved the accuracy of the plans put in, namely, "Plans of part of the town of Newport, and roads connected therewith, in the county of Monmouth;"

"Ground plan of the Westgate Hotel and streets adjoining, in the town of Newport, in the county of Monmouth;" and "Plan of the Canal and Railroads communicating with the town of Newport, Monmouthshire, 1839."

Richard Waters, an attorney, of Newport, who was sworn as a special constable, and stationed at the Westgate Hotel when the attack was made, and Mr. Thomas Latch, identified Mr. Frost as being at the head of the mob when they arrived at the Westgate.

John Rees and James Coles, lads, proved the presence of Frost at Courtybella giving directions to the men.

Thomas Bevan Oliver, a printer of the town, who, as one of the special constables, occupied a position at the front door of the Westgate when the demand was made for a surrender of prisoners.

Henry Evans, a saddler, and Daniel Evans, a tailor, living next door to each other, and nearly opposite to the Westgate, described what they saw from their residence.

The next witness was William Adams, a park-keeper to Sir Charles Morgan, who saw Frost, after the discomfiture of his followers, take refuge in a copse near the lodge.

Sir Thomas Phillips, the Mayor of the Borough, was examined at some length as to the measures he took for the protection of the town, the directions he gave to the soldiers, and the manner in which he was himself wounded.

Edward Hopkins, Superintendent of Police, produced a gun, a sword, some pikes, and a number of staves, spears, long iron rods, mandrils, and picks that were picked up in front of the Westgate after the rioters had dispersed. [The production of the weapons produced a strong sensation in the Court.]

Captain Basil Grey gave a very lucid account of what came under his notice in the course of the affair.

Sergeant James Daily was next called. He was described as a Sergeant of Her Majesty's 45th Regiment of Foot, abiding at the Barracks at Pillgwenlly, in the parish of St. Woolos, in the town of Newport, in the county of Monmouth. A second list furnished to prisoner's counsel described him as abiding at the Newport Poor House. He proved that he had never been stationed at Pillgwenlly, although a part of the Regiment had occupied the Barracks there after the Riot.

The Lord Chief Justice, on the objection of Sir Frederick Pollock, decided that the description was over particular, and the over particularity might mislead.

The evidence of this witness was therefore rejected.

Thomas Walker stated that he and a man named Richard Webb were sent on horseback by the Mayor to glean information as to the movements of the Chartists. At Risca witness fell in with a number of men, and was wounded by them.

CHARTIST RIOTS.

The examination of this witness concluded the proceedings of the third day.

On Friday, 3rd January, the witnesses examined were those named below.

Matthew Williams, a quarryman, living at Argoed, stated that he was forced under threats to get up from his bed and join the rioters. He was told that they would meet Mr. Frost at the Welsh Oak, and when they arrived at that place he saw Mr. Frost.

James Hodge, of Blackwood, who was taken into custody as one of the rioters, described what took place in the presence of Mr. Frost at the Coach and Horses, Blackwood, on Sunday night, November 3rd; his march towards Newport, and his escape across the fields at Pye Corner.

George Lloyd, of Coalbrook Vale, deposed to the proceedings of Zephaniah Williams and his compulsory march with him from the Hills towards Newport; his several attempts to escape, and his being thrown into the canal at Abercarn.

James James, a miner, accompanied Zephaniah Williams and his party from Nantyglo to Newport, so far as Stow Church, where he met a number of people hastily returning. He turned back with them, and went home.

James Samuel, landlord of the Coach and Horses, Llanhilleth, proved that the Chartists visited his house during the night, that Williams was with them, and that for his accommodation he had a tram prepared to convey him towards Newport.

Henry Smith proved driving the tram in which Williams rode with a number of other people.

William Howell, Blaina, deposed to men being provided with arms at the Lodge-room at Zephaniah Williams's house.

James Woodford, gamekeeper at Abercarn, proved that the Chartists robbed his house of guns, pistols, etc., on the Sunday night or Monday morning.

Joseph Anthony, Tydee, narrated the conduct of Zephaniah Williams and his band when they arrived at Tydee.

John Nicholl Hawkins, surgeon, of Newport, who spoke to Zephaniah Williams at Pye Corner, and told him there were soldiers in the town, was next examined.

The evidence of John Parsons, butcher, of Pill, who watched Williams at the rear of 4,000 or 5,000 men pass Stow Churchyard; Thomas Saunders, of Tynycwm, farmer, in whose house and barn Williams and some of his followers took shelter during the night; and Mr. Barnabas Brough, who was taken prisoner by Jones's force at Croes-y-Ceilog, concluded the proceedings of the day.

On Saturday, January 4th, the evidence for the prosecution was completed by the examination of the following witnesses :—

CHARTIST RIOTS.

Mr. Thomas Watkins, the companion of Mr. Barnabas Brough.

John Harford and William Harris, colliers, of Blackwood, who were both apprehended on a charge of high treason, and afterwards volunteered to give evidence.

James Emery, cabinetmaker, of Pontypool, who detailed Jones's proceedings at Abersychan.

John Parry, labourer, of Pontnewynydd.

William Ainsell, collier, of Abersychan, proved what transpired at Jones's Beerhouse, Pontypool, on the eventful night.

John Phillips, described as of Croes-y-Ceilog, in the parish of Llanfrechfa, was proved as living about 60 yards nearer Newport than the Lower Cocks Public-house.

The objection of Sir Frederick Pollock as to the insufficiency of the description was allowed by the Court, and the evidence of the witness was therefore excluded.

Christopher Kidner, butcher, near Croes-y-ceilog, and John Matthews, gardener at Malpas Court, traced Jones's division through Malpas, and up the lane to Penylan.

Richard Pugh and Edmund Lloyd, landlords respectively of the Coach and Horses and Royal Oak, Blackwood, were next placed in the box.

Joseph Stockdale spoke to some conversation he had had with Zephaniah Williams at his house on the Sunday evening prior to the meeting on the mountain.

William Henry Williams, an accountant, of Newport, was examined as to the dealings in gunpowder of Mr. Crossfield, a merchant of the town.

Moses Scard, one of the Borough Police Force, produced some pikes and other weapons which he picked up after the mob had fled from the Westgate. He collected 150.

Thomas Watts, of Gellygroes, deposed to meeting from 8,000 to 10,000 men at Pye Corner, moving in all directions, and observing from 200 to 300 pikes and mandrils and guns lying on the ground.

Morgan James, described as of Pillgwenlly, in the parish of St. Woolos, in the borough of Newport, in the county of Monmouth, collier, sometimes abiding at the house of his son, John James, in the parish of Bedwellty, in the county of Monmouth, collier, was called.

Sir Frederick Pollock objected to the description.

The objection was argued at length by the Lord Chief Justice and his brother Judges. Several gave their opinion that the description, taken as a whole, was inaccurate, and the witness was not therefore examined.

The last witness examined was Mr. Thomas Jones Phillips, solicitor, who apprehended Frost; and Mr. Phillips's evidence closed the case for the prosecution.

COUNSEL'S ADDRESS FOR THE DEFENCE.

On the following Monday morning Sir Frederick Pollock commenced his address for the defence. After paying a well-deserved compliment to the Judges for their unexampled patience and moderation, and to the jury for their great attention and forbearance during the protracted trial, he directed attention to the point upon which the case against the prisoner chiefly rested— namely, whether the proceeding of Sunday, 3rd November, which terminated in the fatal transaction of Monday morning (fatal only to the persons who were unfortunately engaged in that transaction), was done for any treasonable purpose—criminal he admitted it was—and was that treasonable purpose existing in the mind of Mr. Frost at the time he concerted the proceeding; at the time that he joined and marched with the persons from the Welsh Oak down to the corner of the Westgate Hotel, where he quitted them. He contended that the case against the prisoner—omitting certain declarations attributed to him—was, as a case of treason, absolutely nothing. He did not forget the crime committed in the assembling and marching of those persons; but, without those declarations alleged to have been by the prisoner, the case of treason was absolutely nothing. When the mob arrived at the Westgate, it was alleged that they made to the special constables a demand in the following words : "Surrender yourselves our prisoners." Although this was a most important fact, yet it was spoken to by only one witness. It was singular that this first act—this parley, this demand, before any violence was used, before a shot was fired, before a window was broken—was not distinctly proved over and over again. In reply to that challenge, one of their own party was said to have called out, "Never!" Where was that person? Had he been sought out? It could not be said that he was among the slain? Why was he not forthcoming? The learned counsel suggested that the words used were, "Surrender our prisoners," meaning the persons that were then known to be in the room—Chartists who had been apprehended in the course of the night—and he was instructed that several witnesses would be called to prove that this was so. The learned counsel next dwelt upon the project of blowing up the Bridge, and stopping the Mails, and pointing out the inutility of the proceeding in furthering the scheme alleged against the prisoner, inasmuch as if the bags were stopped at Newport, the Mail from Bristol and other places in the West of England would be carried on to Birmingham and the North as usual. This was the most absurd, inconsistent—nay, impossible—of all charges that ever was presented to the consideration of an intelligent jury, on which to fix upon the prisoner a crime of so important a character. After remarking upon the discrepancies in the statements of several witnesses, and giving an ingenious turn to expressions used by them, he proceeded to glance at what he had no doubt was the true character of the whole proceeding. Vincent had been tried for sedition, and was then in prison. He was considered by the general body of the Chartists as a martyr to the cause which they espoused, and for that reason meetings were held. A statement appeared in a paper published in Monmouth giving a character to the meeting as if the parties had assembled expressing a determination to rescue Vincent out of the Gaol at Monmouth. At the meeting referred to, it had been contemplated by the large body of ignorant men up among the Hills that such a scheme was possible. Mr. Frost deprecated the use of any such violence; but advocated, or rather permitted, them to march to Newport that they might not in desperation take some course that would be fatal to the public peace. With intentions truly peaceful they were permitted to go to Newport with the single purpose of "showing their appearance" and strength, prior to making another appeal to the magistrates, either in favour of Vincent having the term of his imprisonment altered, or the supposed character of his confinement changed to a system less rigorous and severe. With regard to the mob firing upon the Military, the learned counsel argued at length that Mr. Frost could not know, and did not know, that any soldiers were at the Westgate; that the Mayor and Sergeant Daily were wounded at the moment of opening the shutters; and that the instant the shutters were opened and the soldiers fired upon the mob, the mob threw down their weapons and took to flight. No sort of resistance was made after that. From the personal conduct and character of Frost; from the fact that he had a wife and five daughters and a son in Newport, and from minor circumstances, he asked the jury to believe the improbability of his being engaged in or having contemplated the serious consequences which resulted from the proceedings of those with whom he had associated. In conclusion, he observed that the rest of England would hardly believe the quiet, the peace, and security in which the proceedings at Monmouth had been conducted. Where there was the remotest suspicion of treason existing in the country among persons, to some extent armed and capable of combining in large numbers, it was quite right that the high authorities of the law should be protected, and that the peace of the town where justice was to be administered should be secured by the unusual presence of soldiers for that purpose, but their services had been altogether superfluous.

Witnesses for the defence were then called.

John Wilton, lathmaker, and William Frost, labourer, both Chartists, were examined and cross-examined at some length. The chief point in their evidence was that they gathered from observations made by the mob as they passed down Stow Hill that they were going to the Westgate for their prisoners—namely, the Chartists who had been taken into custody during the night.

CHARTIST RIOTS.

Benjamin Gould, painter and glazier, and a borough constable, swore that, in reply to the Superintendent of Police, when the leaders of the mob came to the front door of the Westgate, one of them said, "We want our prisoners."

Edward Patten, a carpenter, attributed to those who made the demand a little more respectful language. His version of the words was, "Would they please to give up the prisoners they had got or taken before daylight."

Joshua Thomas, carpenter, was called to rebut the statement of one of the witnesses for the prosecution, that a body of the Chartists passed up Commercial Street to the Westgate.

The Rev. Charles Coles, one of the magistrates of the county of Monmouth, and Capel Hanbury Leigh, Esq., Lord-Lieutenant of the County, were called to prove that Mr. Frost had applied to them in reference to the case of Vincent. The applications to each were similarly worded.

Edward Thomas, grocer, tallow-chandler, and draper, stated the mode of conveying the Mails from Newport to Bristol. He admitted that he had been a Chartist for ten months, but he knew nothing of any meeting having been called in Newport on the 4th November in reference to Vincent.

William Townsend, iron merchant, spoke favourably of Mr. Frost's character. [This witness's son was apprehended with Vincent, but he denied having said that, if sufficiently well at the time, he would have sacrificed his life rather than allow them to be taken.]

The last witness of the day was Sir Benjamin Hall, Bart., M.P. (afterwards Lord Llanover), who had known Mr. Frost from 1831 to 1834, and had never heard anything against him.

On the following day—Tuesday—two witnesses were called to prove that certain acceptances of Mr. Frost, which arrived at maturity at the time of the Riots, were duly paid.

Another witness—Henry Williams, who acted as *aide-de-camp*—stated that the demand made by the leaders of the mob at the door of the Westgate was in these words, "Surrender up your prisoners."

The Right Hon. Lord Granville Somerset, M.P. for Monmouthshire, was sworn, and stated that in the spring of 1831, when a candidate for the representation of the county, Mr. Frost protected him from the violence of a crowd when canvassing at Newport.

Edward Hopkins, Superintendent of Police, was called, but having been previously called to produce the weapons found by him, his evidence was objected to. After a long argument, the Court sanctioned the following question being put to him: "Did you ask any of the mob on the 4th of November what they wanted?" To which he replied, "I did not."

After this, Sir F. Pollock, in order to preserve the right which the law allowed, said a few words to the jury, when

Mr. Kelly, the prisoner's second counsel, commented upon the whole case, assuming great confidence of the prisoner's innocence of the serious charge upon which he was indicted. He quoted the law of Edward III., by which all treasons were defined; and declaimed, with much force of language, upon the corruption of Judges, and the weakness and servility of juries, who, in the time of Henry VIII., grossly and mischievously perverted that statute, and allowed the doctrine of "constructive treason" to creep in. That doctrine had laid the foundation for the body of law which now existed upon the subject, and they were to be guided and governed by it as a precedent. With ample illustration of previous cases, Mr. Kelly pursued the line of defence set forth by his leader, that however serious the crime which Mr. Frost had perpetrated, it could not be brought within the law of high treason; and, with great severity, he condemned the contradiction and perjuries sworn to by some of the witnesses for the prosecution.

At the conclusion of the learned counsel's address,

The Lord Chief Justice said: John Frost, now is the proper time for you to be heard, if you wish to address anything to the gentlemen of the jury beyond what your learned counsel has said. You will not be allowed to be heard after the Solicitor-General has closed the case on the part of the prosecution.

John Frost: My Lord, I am so well satisfied with what my counsel have said, that I decline saying anything upon this occasion.

The Solicitor-General at once proceeded to reply upon the whole case, and complained of the appeal which prisoner's counsel had made to the feelings of the jury, and to the prejudice which he sought to implant in their minds by terming it a Crown prosecution. He repeated that the charge which it was his duty to make against the prisoner was that, prior to the 4th of November, he believed there were large bodies of men in different parts of the country who were inclined to rise and rebel against the Government; that he raised a large body of armed men to march into Newport, intending either by surprise or terror, from the number of those men and their arms, to prevent resistance, or by force to overcome that resistance, and take possession of the town of Newport; that he intended to supersede the magistracy and the law, and himself to exercise authority there; and that he intended to make the taking of the town of Newport a signal to other parts of the country to rise into rebellion, and thereby to change the Constitution.

The speech of the Solicitor-General was not concluded until the following day—Wednesday, January 8th.

The Lord Chief Justice, in summing up, commenced by explaining the law of High Treason. He observed that if the outline made by the Officers of the Crown was filled up, there was no doubt whatever that the guilt of the party accused amounted to high treason; and, on the other hand, if falling short of that offence, it amounted to no more than a very aggravated misdemeanor, and upon that supposition and state of facts the prisoner would be entitled to an acquittal. The whole evidence, as it appeared upon his Lordship's notes, was then recapitulated. His Lordship subsequently directed particular attention to the several transactions in which, from the evidence of the witnesses, Mr. Frost appeared to have been engaged on the Sunday night and Monday morning, and also to the declarations alleged to have been made by him. Reminding the jury that they must be satisfied that the Crown had by clear and conclusive testimony supported the charge made against the prisoner, he left the case in their hands, relying upon their judgment and their conscience, being certain that they would come to that conclusion which the truth and justice of the case required.

The jury retired at twenty-five minutes before six o'clock, and returned into Court at five minutes past six, and found the prisoner Guilty, the foreman adding, " My Lord, we wish to recommend the prisoner to the merciful consideration of the Court."

The Lord Chief Justice said he would forward the recommendation to the proper quarter.

TRIAL OF WILLIAMS AND JONES.

On the day following that on which the verdict was returned against Frost—Thursday, the 9th January—the Court proceeded with the trial of Zephaniah Williams; and on Monday, January 13th, the jury returned a verdict of Guilty, accompanied with a recommendation to mercy.

William Jones was next put upon his trial, and on the 15th—Wednesday—the jury returned a similar verdict.

On the same day Mr. Stone, having been assigned as counsel, together with Mr. Skinner, for Charles Waters, Jenkin Morgan, John Rees, Richard Benfield, and John Lovett, applied to the Court that the prisoners named might be brought to the bar for the purpose of withdrawing their plea of not guilty, and pleading guilty. They were, therefore, brought to the bar, and, having severally pleaded guilty, were then removed.

ACQUITTALS.

The Attorney-General then moved that George Turner, otherwise George Cole, Solomon Brittan, James Aust, and Edmund Edmunds be brought to the bar. This having been done, and the jury formally charged with the prisoners, the Attorney-General stated that he did not intend to press the prosecution against any of these prisoners, inasmuch as it appeared, with regard to Solomon Brittan and George Turner, that a question might arise with respect to their identity; and that with regard to James Aust and Edmunds, there was some reason to doubt whether, in joining with the insurgents, they had acted voluntarily.

Under the direction of the Court, the jury thereupon returned a verdict of Not Guilty.

SENTENCE UPON FROST, WILLIAMS, AND JONES.

On Thursday, January 16th, John Frost, Zephaniah Williams, and William Jones were placed at the bar; and John Frost being asked by the Clerk of Arraigns what he had to say why the Court should not give him judgment to die, according to law.

Mr. Geach, in the absence of the other counsel, applied to the Court under the following circumstances:—There was a ground upon which they intended to move in arrest of judgment, the ground being that upon the jury who tried Mr. Frost there was a juryman, unable to read or write, who answered to the name of Christopher John. The real name of the juryman was John Christopher. There was also on the list another person named John Christopher. Against any persons answering to the name of Christopher it had been arranged to object; but with regard to Christopher John, they had succeeded in obtaining no information, and they did not feel justified therefore in objecting to the person answering to this name when called.

The Court, having considered the matter and referred to a case directly in point (12th East., known as the Juryman Case), decided that at most it was only a cause of challenge; and that it was perfectly clear the only time an objection could be made was upon the juryman being sworn.

Zephaniah Williams and William Jones were then severally asked by the Clerk of Arraigns, "What have you to say for yourself why the Court should not give you judgment to die, according to law?"

The Lord Chief Justice, in addressing the prisoners, held out no hope of mercy, and passed the sentence of the Court in the following words:—"That you John Frost, and you Zephaniah Williams, and you William Jones be taken hence to the place from whence you came, and be thence drawn on a hurdle to the place of execution, and that each of you be there hanged by the neck until you be dead, and that afterwards the head of each of you shall be severed from his body, and the body of each divided into four quarters shall be disposed of as Her Majesty shall think fit. And may God Almighty have mercy upon your souls!"

The prisoners received the announcement of their fate with the utmost firmness and propriety of demeanor, and were the only persons in the Court whom the fearful nature of the sentence did not affect.

CHARTIST RIOTS.

A similar sentence was subsequently passed upon Charles Waters, John Lovett, Richard Benfield, John Rees, and Jenkin Morgan.

The Lord Chief Justice intimated, however, that as they had not been the contrivers of the treason, their lives would be spared, but that they would be banished from their country for the remainder of their lives.

MISCELLANEOUS CHARGES.

The Calendar of the period gives the result of the other cases tried, as follows, the offences being " Treason " and "Sedition " when not otherwise stated :—

John Partridge, 44, pleaded guilty, six months' hard labour; sedition and conspiracy.

James Aust, 25, acquitted.

Thomas Davies, 33, acquitted.

Amy Meredith, 45; James Meredith, 11; and Thomas Kay were charged with breaking open the dwelling-house of John Jones, and stealing bread and cheese and a six-gallon cask of beer, at Trevethin; acquitted.

William Williams, 29, breaking open the house of John Lloyd, Bedwellty, armed with spears, etc., and threatening Ann Walters, and taking from her a quantity of rum, gin, and beer; discharged by proclamation.

Solomon Britton, 23, acquitted.

George George, 37, six months' hard labour, for burglary.

George Turner, *alias* Cole, 37, acquitted.

William Shellard, 36, traversed; afterwards sentenced at the March Assizes to 18 months' hard labour.

Edmund Edmunds, 34, acquitted.

Samuel Etheridge, 61, acquitted.

John Lewis Llewellin, 49, traversed.

Evan Edwards, 24, one month; making bullets.

Benjamin Richards, 41, six months.

Thomas Llewellin, 44, six months' hard labour.

Thomas Morgan, 26, entering the house of William Adams, of Ebbw Vale, and with threats compelling Thomas Williams to join in an unlawful confederacy; three months.

Moses Horner, 21; William Horner, 18; and Thomas Davies, 25; stealing at Mynyddislwyn a shot belt, 3lb. of shot, and a dagger, the property of William Thomas; traversed.

Thomas Edwards, 28, six months' hard labour; William John Llewellin, 29, one year; Job Harris, 28, two months; and Joseph Coles; burglariously entering the house of John Walters and assaulting him, at Bedwellty.

Lewis Rowland, 37, one year.

John Owen, 28, six months.

John Batten (the younger), 18, conspiracy; discharged.

Isaac Phillips, 18, stealing a cleaver, the property of Charles Harris, of Machen; discharged.

William Jones, 25, conspiracy ; discharged.
John Gibby, 30, one year.
Edward Frost, conspiracy ; discharged.
John Fisher, discharged.
William Davies, discharged.
Ebenezer Williams, discharged.
Thomas Lewis, 33, three months ; Edmund Richards, 39, three months ; James Moore, 20, twelve months ; for riotously assembling at Trevethin.
Edward Pillinger, 28, rioting at Risca ; discharged.
George Thompson, riotously assembling at Trevethin ; discharged.
Thomas Davies, ditto, four months.
Charles Bucknell, ditto, acquitted.
Frederick Turner, ditto, recognizances forfeited ; afterwards discharged.
Isaac Davies, ditto, acquitted.
Henry Harris, ditto, discharged.
Thomas Bolton, ditto, acquitted.
David Williams, ditto, recognizances estreated.
John Charles, ditto, three months ; riotous assembly.
William Havard, ditto, two months.
Thomas Ball, ditto, acquitted ; riotously assembling at Trevethin.

OPINION OF THE JUDGES.

A case prepared by the Lord Chief Justice for the opinion of the Judges upon the question reserved at the trials with respect to the delivery of the list of witnesses against Frost, Williams, and Jones, was argued before all the fifteen Judges in the Court of Exchequer, upon the 25th, 27th, and 28th January, when Sir Frederick Pollock was heard on behalf of John Frost, the Attorney-General was heard on behalf of the Crown, and Sir Frederick Pollock was heard in reply.

Mr. Kelly was heard on behalf of Zephaniah Williams, Sir William Follett on behalf of William Jones, the Attorney-General on behalf of the Crown, and the respective counsel for the prisoners were heard in reply.

At the conclusion of the argument, the decision of the Judges was communicated by Lord Chief Justice Tindal to the Secretary of State for the Home Department.

The Judges determined that the conviction was right.

SIR JOHN CAMPBELL'S OPINION.

After the trials were concluded, Sir John Campbell placed the following remarks in his Diary, which has since been published :—
"I have passed a very anxious day, as if I myself had been on trial. To my utter astonishment and dismay, Tindal summed up

CHARTIST RIOTS.

for an acquittal. What he meant, the Lord only knows. No human being doubted the guilt of the accused, and we had proved it by the clearest evidence. Chief Justice Tindal is a very honourable man, and had no assignable reason for deviating from the right course. Yet from the beginning to the end of his charge he laboured for an acquittal."

REMISSION OF THE CAPITAL SENTENCE.

A large number of petitions from different parts of the country were presented to the Government on the prisoners' behalf ; and on Saturday, February 1st, Her Majesty was graciously pleased to remit the capital sentences, upon the condition of the prisoners being transported for the term of their natural lives.

REMOVAL OF THE PRISONERS FROM MONMOUTH.

On Sunday night, 2nd February, the prisoners, in very stormy weather, were removed from Monmouth Gaol, and, under military escort, conveyed to Chepstow, and placed on board the *Usk* steamer, which left at six o'clock on Monday morning, bound for Portsmouth, at which place they were put on board convict hulks.

From Chepstow the *Usk* proceeded to Kingroad, and took in coals and provisions ; and subsequently, owing to stress of weather, she put into Ilfracombe, where she lay for 48 hours. On the 7th she put into Padstow. Arriving at Portsmouth on Saturday, the 15th, after a passage of thirteen days, the prisoners were immediately transferred to the *York* hulk, and clothed in convict apparel.

Frost felt his position keenly, and wept bitterly ; Williams appeared to exhibit no particular emotion ; and Jones was indifferent throughout the voyage, repeatedly expressing a wish that the vessel would sink with all on board.

On February 24th, Frost, Williams, and Jones embarked on board the *Mandarin* convict ship, at Spithead, with 210 other convicts. On the 26th the vessel put into Falmouth, with loss of topmast. From this place Frost wrote to his wife, begging her not to leave England to follow him, but in her care for her children to show her affection for her husband.

DESTINATION OF THE PRISONERS.

The prisoners were conveyed to Van Dieman's Land. Frost employed some years of his time as a schoolmaster ; Jones followed his occupation of a watchmaker; whilst Zephaniah Williams turned his attention to the minerals of the Colony, and became a prosperous coalowner.

IN MEMORIAM.

On Flowering Sunday—April 12th, 1840—the graves of the Chartists slain at the Westgate on the 4th November were decked

MONMOUTH GAOL.

with flowers and laurels, and surmounted by the following lines :—

"May the rose of England never blow,
The Clyde of Scotland cease to flow,
The harp of Ireland never play,
Until the Chartists gain the day."

THE PRISONERS AFTERWARDS PARDONED.

After repeated agitation, the Government, in 1854, granted the prisoners a pardon, not to return to the United Kingdom.

Mr. Frost took up his residence in the United States, and, by publication of fierce letters in the Press, made himself obnoxious to the Home Government. Memorials, however, from Sheffield, Newport, and other towns were repeatedly sent to the Government praying for Frost's unconditional pardon; and this was granted in 1856. Frost arrived in Liverpool, and at once made known his intention of giving a series of political lectures. In August he returned to Newport—his native place—and was received by an enthusiastic and admiring crowd. He addressed them in language which at once alienated him from many persons who would otherwise have been disposed to extend to him their sympathy; and his remarks were likened, in the London Press, to the ravings of a madman. Frost lost no time in demanding the restitution of his rights as a freeman of the Borough of Newport; and the persistency of his demand led the Town Council to a consideration of his claim, when they decided that, although Her Majesty's free pardon restored him all rights formerly possessed by him, he was not a burgess in occupation, through non-residence, and therefore not entitled to have his name published in the list of freemen.

Frost had taken up his residence at Stapleton, near Bristol, where he found his wife living on his return to England. She died in 1875, and the old man resolved to die there too. A daughter remained to him whom he regarded as the only solace of his life. He was simple in his habits, and for many years lived as a total abstainer from intoxicating drinks.

In a letter to the STAR OF GWENT in January, 1861, Frost stated, "It is my intention to begin, in a very short time, my autobiography. There are some things in my eventful life which I should be very sorry to carry with me to the grave. I shall give an account of the rise and progress of the affair in Wales in 1839, and the apparent cause of its sudden termination; what took place from the dispersion of the people in Newport till I was apprehended and secured in Monmouth Gaol; what took place during my confinement in the Gaol till the trial; the twenty-three days' confinement in the condemned cell," &c., &c. No such account, however, was published, and, probably, Mr. Frost never seriously set about its composition.

John Frost, after years of great seclusion, passed away in his cottage at Stapleton, on Saturday, July 28th, 1877, at the ripe old age of 93 years.

William Lloyd Jones died in December, 1873, at Launceston, Australia, from which colony he had no desire to depart.

Zephaniah Williams died on the 8th May, 1874, at Tasmania.

REVIEW OF THE TRIAL, &c.

Mr. W. Townsend, M.A., Q.C., Recorder of Macclesfield, in his work entitled "Modern State Trials" (Longman, 1850, two vols., 8vo.), gives a very graphic description of these trials, and points out, with a critical and legal eye, some peculiarities connected with them. Sir John Campbell, the then Attorney-General, became a Peer of the Realm, and Chief Justice of the Queen's Bench. Sir Thomas Wilde, the Solicitor-General, also became a Peer of the Realm, and was Lord High Chancellor. Mr. Wightman and Mr. Talfourd, associated with them, were both raised to the Judicial Bench, the latter suddenly dying while in the act of charging a grand jury at Stafford at the Spring Assizes of 1854. Sir Frederick Pollock, the prisoners' leading counsel, was subsequently Chief Baron of the Exchequer; Mr. Kelly, who was associated with him in the trials, became Solicitor-General, but lost office on the break-up of Sir Robert Peel's Administration; and, although remaining plain Sir Fitzroy Kelly, he occupied a splendid position at the bar.

In "Blackwood's Magazine," 1850, a review of Mr. Townsend's work by Mr. Samuel Warren, Q.C., is published. It concludes with the following remarks:—"Have they (the prisoners) ever appreciated the skill and vigilance with which they were defended? It is true that the one chance objection—which is wonderful should have occurred to any at all—was ultimately pronounced only by a majority of the Judges, after lengthened debate, to have been taken too late; but if it had not occurred to the vigilant advocate when it did—if no one had taken it at any time—would not the traitors have been executed? Unquestionably public justice, the public safety, required it. Whether Sir Frederick Pollock purposely delayed making the objection till the moment when he did—and the Attorney-General insinuated before the fifteen Judges that such was the case—thinking that course more advantageous to the prisoner, or whether the objection had not in fact occurred to him till it was too late, we do not profess to say."

PRESENTATION TO SIR THOMAS PHILLIPS.

The conduct of Sir Thomas Phillips during his mayoralty was considered deserving the hearty recognition of his fellow-townsmen, and a movement set on foot to present him with a testimonial was warmly supported. The presentation was made on the 24th

CHARTIST RIOTS.

September, 1840, at a meeting held at the Girls' National School, over which Mr. R. J. Blewitt, the representative of the Monmouth Boroughs, presided. The testimonial, which was subscribed to by upwards of 600 persons, consisted of a magnificent service of silver plate, upon which was an inscription intimating that it was presented to Sir Thomas Phillips in testimony of their high admiration of the foresight and firmness displayed by him during his mayoralty at Newport, Mon., in 1839, and especially during the night of the 3rd November and the morning of the 4th, whereby he was enabled, under Divine Providence, to frustrate the treasonable design against the Constitution, and to deliver the town and country from imminent danger.

SIR THOMAS PHILLIPS.

CHARTIST ANECDOTES.

John Frost was a firm believer in the special interposition of Divine Providence, and related to a friend two anecdotes in confirmation of his belief as directly applying to himself. He said that after he and Jones and Williams were taken back to prison subsequent to the fearful sentence of hanging, drawing, and quartering being passed upon them, Williams and Jones proposed to him that they should all commit suicide, to avoid the shameful death from which there seemed to be no escape. He at first objected, but subsequently wavered in his mind, and kneeling down in his cell, he prayed fervently to the Almighty to guide him aright. An inspiration came over him, he said, like a dream, and he felt strong in the belief that suicide would be the wrong course to take. "I told them," said he, "it would be a cowardly act, and I begged of them not to think of it. They gave way after some difficulty, and we all lived to thank God for putting it into our hearts."

SAVED BY A DREAM.

Mr. Frost, when in the United States, filled the office of schoolmaster, and had occasion to go from one part of the district to another, across the mountains many miles away. On taking his seat in the coach, prior to starting on one occasion, a young Scotchwoman, daughter of the mother of one of his pupils, rushed up to the vehicle in a state of excitement, and implored him not to go the proposed journey. He asked her why, and she said she had dreamed the night before that the coach was attacked by freebooters on the way, and that all the passengers were murdered. He smiled at her fears, and tried to calm them; but she still persisted, and begged him on her knees to listen to the warning she gave, assuring him, with tears in her eyes, that if he went he would never reach the end of his journey alive. "At last," said he, "I gave way, and jumped out of the coach, and the poor girl was joyful enough, notwithstanding that I laughed at her foolish fancies a good deal." A few days afterwards, he went on to relate, the news came that the coach was attacked on the road, and every passenger killed. "Yes," said the old man earnestly, "I am a firm believer in the special interposition of a Divine Providence."

CHARTIST HAT.

Mr. W. Watkins, hatter, of Commercial Street, has preserved as a curiosity a cap which he obtained from the late Mr. S. T. Hallen, landlord of the Westgate. The hat was picked up after the flight of the Chartists. In shape it is like a jockey's cap, with stout leather peak. The outer covering is of green plaid serge, and it is lined with coarse canvas. Between the outer covering and the lining is a frame of hoop iron, composed of a circle to fit the size of the head, and four semi-circular pieces rivetted together, and forming a dome shape. The cap weighs $3\frac{1}{2}$lbs.

REMINISCENCES BY DR. PRICE, LLANTRISSENT.

In a biographical notice of this eccentric person, the following reminiscences of the Chartist Riots are given:—"In the Chartist movement I took a very active interest. I was appointed the leader of the Pontypridd district. The other prominent persons were Frost, Zephaniah Williams, and William Jones. Jones was a thorough good fellow; but I had not so good an opinion of Frost. I remember that six weeks before the Chartist Riots he sent for the delegates to meet him at Twyn-y-Star, Blaenau Gwent. I went there as the delegate from the Merthyr and Aberdare districts. Frost, who was chairman, said, 'I have called you together to ask will you rise at my bidding? for it must be done.' Well, upon that, one of the delegates—an old soldier named David Davies, who had served for 25 years in the Army, and had fought in the battle of Waterloo—got up and said, 'I will tell you, Mr. Frost, the condition upon which my lodge will rise, and there is no other condition, as far as I am concerned. The Abersychan Lodge is 1,600 strong; 1,200 of them are old soldiers; the remaining 400 have never handled arms, but we can turn them into fighting men in no time. I have been sent here to tell you that we shall not rise until you give us a list of those we have to remove—to kill.' Every delegate gave a similar reply, and Frost promised that he would not call them up until he had given them the list asked for. That meeting lasted until two or three o'clock in the morning. In about six weeks afterwards, on a Saturday night, Frost sent a person, named Isaac Morgan, to me with a request that I should see him early on the following morning. I obeyed the summons, and when I saw him Frost had a shy distrustful look which I did not at all like. He led me into a well-furnished apartment, and there, behind the door, stood a large screen some six or seven feet high. Frost continually cast his eye in the direction of the screen, so I at once suspected that he had some concealed there. I did not say anything, however; but took care to converse in a low whisper, so that my voice could not be heard at the other side of the room. I took hold of Frost by the coat, and pulled him gently towards the window, and there I asked him why he had sent for me. 'Have you not heard?' said he. 'I have heard nothing after the Twyn-y-Star meeting,' I answered. 'Well,' he said, 'we are going to rise this night week, and I want to know whether you will meet us here.' 'Where is your plan?' I asked. 'I will not budge until I have everything explained.' He said that the plan was in the printing office of Mr. Etheridge.* I then asked for the original, but he could not produce it; and I refused to agree to anything except what had been decided at the Twyn-y-Star meeting. 'What,' said he, do you want us to kill the soldiers—kill a thousand of them in one night?' 'Yes,' I said, 'a hundred thousand, if it is necessary.' 'Dear me,' cried he, 'I cannot do it! I cannot do it!' and then he cried like a child, and talked about heaven and hell. I cursed him, and said, 'You shall not put a sword in my hand and a rope around my neck at the same time.' I then left him. The rising took place, as he said it would, but no one from Merthyr or the Aberdare district took part in it."

---

* Etheridge was a printer in Newport, who had an office in the rear of High Street, near the Greyhound Inn. He is said to have "farmed" the poor, at the Refuge, at so much per head; and built the house in Market Street, with iron pillars in front of it, for the purpose of a Liberal Reading-room. This has recently been pulled down.

CHARTIST RIOTS.

DISCOVERY OF BULLETS.

On the removal, on September 17th, 1884, of the wood pillars which supported the porch in front of the Old Westgate, there were found four roughly-made bullets or slugs, which had evidently lain in the interior of the pillars since the day of the attack on the building—forty-five years before.

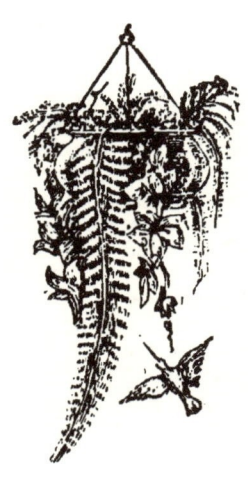

www.ingramcontent.com/pod-product-compliance
Lightning Source LLC
Chambersburg PA
CBHW020332090426
42735CB00009B/1503